WORD
BIBLICAL
THEMES

WORD
BIBLICAL
THEMES

---

2 Peter–Jude

RICHARD J. BAUCKHAM

ZONDERVAN
ACADEMIC

ZONDERVAN ACADEMIC

2 Peter, Jude
Copyright © 1990 by Word, Incorporated

Requests for information should be addressed to:
Zondervan, *3900 Sparks Dr. SE, Grand Rapids, Michigan 49546*

ISBN 978-0-310-11494-9 (softcover)

Library of Congress Cataloging-in-Publication Data

Bauckham, Richard.
      Jude, 2 Peter: Richard J. Bauckham.
         p. cm.
      Includes bibliographical references.
      ISBN 978-0-849-92792-0
      1. Bible. N.T. Jude—Criticism, interpretation, etc. 2. Bible. N.T. Peter, 2nd—
Criticism, interpretation, etc. I. Title. II. Title: Jude, Second Peter. III. Series.
BS2815.2.B38 1990
227'.9306—dc20   89-49676

Scripture quotations in this volume from Jude and 2 Peter are from the author's translation in *Jude, 2 Peter*, Volume 50, of the Word Biblical abbreviations for the other versions used in this volume.

Any internet addresses (websites, blogs, etc.) and telephone numbers in this book are offered as a resource. They are not intended in any way to be or imply an endorsement by Zondervan, nor does Zondervan vouch for the content of these sites and numbers for the life of this book.

Printed in the United States of America

HB 01.06.2023

IN MEMORY OF
Colin Hemer
distinguished New Testament scholar
and Christian friend to many
who died on 14 June 1987

CONTENTS

FOREWORD

Finding the great themes of the books of the Bible is essential to the study of God's Word, and to the preaching and teaching of its truths. But these themes or ideas are often like precious gems; they lie beneath the surface and can only be discovered with some difficulty. The large commentaries are most useful to this discovery process, but they are not usually designed to help the student trace the important subjects within a given book of Scripture.

The Word Biblical Themes meet this need by bringing together, within a few pages, all of what is contained in a biblical volume on the subjects that are thought to be most significant to that volume. A companion series to the Word Biblical Commentary, these books seek to distill the theological essence of the biblical books as interpreted in the more technical series and to serve it up in ways that will enrich the preaching, teaching, worship, and discipleship of God's people.

The two letters which carry the names of Jude and 2 Peter in our Bibles are not everyone's immediate favorites, and both devotional and scholarly study has tended to overlook them.

With Richard Bauckham's edition of the Word Biblical Commentary, Volume 50, this situation has been redressed. And the importance of these two small New Testament books has been brought into prominence once again. Dr. Bauckham's commentary has already been hailed as groundbreaking, as recent literary finds from a Jewish-Christian-gnostic library were pressed into service and Jewish pseudepigraphical books were used to illumine the biblical text. As I mentioned in a survey of recent commentaries (in *New Testament Books for Pastor and Teacher*, Westminster Press, 1984), Bauckham's volume has the rare distinction of being an English-speaking study that is now an international front-runner.

All this accolade should whet the reader's appetite for the fare which Dr. Bauckham has made available in a semi-popular and attractive presentation for the Word Biblical Themes series. This short book will be a much-sought-after addition to any minister's library.

It is sent forth in the hope that it will contribute to the vitality of God's people, renewed by the Word and the Spirit and ever in need of renewal.

The University of Sheffield
Sheffield, England

Ralph P. Martin
New Testament Editor
Word Biblical Themes
Word Biblical Commentary

PREFACE

This volume is based on the detailed exegetical work to be found in my volume in the Word Biblical Commentary, *Jude, 2 Peter*. Where the exegesis and interpretations I offer in this volume are controversial, detailed justification for them, with evidence and interaction with other views, will always be found in that commentary. In this volume I have largely avoided discussion of other interpretations and have concentrated instead on positive exposition of the message of these letters as I learned to understand it in the course of writing my commentary. I hope this will not be taken to be an arrogant disregard for views which differ from my own. The point is simply that I have already considered those views, I hope fairly and usually in detail, in the commentary, and I wished to do something different here. I have also read most of what has been published on these letters since I wrote the commentary, but have found no reason to change the views I expressed before. However, it is only fair to warn the reader that on many points of detailed exegesis and broad interpretation of these letters, on which I state my views in this volume, there is no scholarly consensus. But we must all take the risk of interpreting Scripture to the best of our abilities in the light that has so far fallen on it for us.

There is no biblical translation, however literal, which does not embody many disputed decisions about the interpretation of the text (as well as, of course, the most original form of the text). In this volume I have usually quoted from the translations of Jude and 2 Peter which I published in my commentary. I have taken care to do so especially when my translation differs from the most commonly used translations in a way that is really significant for interpretation. Justifications for my translations appear in the commentary. Other biblical quotations in this volume are usually from the Revised Standard Version.

Jude and 2 Peter have often been treated as letters with a very similar outlook directed to very similar church situations, if not precisely the same situation. But in my commentary I argued that, in spite of the fact that 2 Peter borrows some material from Jude, they are in fact very different works, facing different problems in different ways in different contexts. I have therefore not attempted in this volume to deal with the two letters jointly, but have tried to hear and to convey the distinct message of each separately. Jude is treated before 2 Peter (rather than in the canonical order), because I consider that Jude was written first and was used by the author of 2 Peter.

Neither Jude nor 2 Peter has enjoyed a high reputation in modern biblical scholarship. Many biblical scholars have compared them unfavorably with other New Testament writings, especially the Pauline letters, and some have been openly contemptuous of them. I am convinced that much of this denigration and criticism of Jude and 2 Peter is based on ignorance. Because they have simply accepted a scholarly tradition which regards these works as of little interest or value, many biblical scholars scarcely bother to read them, let alone to study them carefully, to reexamine the forms of interpretation which have become conventional or to attempt a fresh, unprejudiced evaluation.

The attempt, by a strong tradition of modern New Testament scholarship, to set up Paul as a standard of excellence, by which most other New Testament authors fall short to a greater or lesser degree, is to be questioned. The point of the New Testament canon is, in part, its diversity. United in the broad contours of early Christian belief, the various New Testament writings are different in style of thought and expression, reflecting their authors' differing gifts, varied insights and interests, different backgrounds and contexts. They are complementary. If we lacked any of them, our understanding of the apostolic faith and teaching would be to some degree poorer.

No doubt, if we *had* to choose, we should all prefer to be without some than to be without others. But the canon means precisely that we do not have to choose. Our concern should be, not with whether one is more valuable than another, but with the particular contribution each has to make. If we read and study Jude and 2 Peter with this positive concern, we shall discover, as generations of Christians have before us, two of the many scriptural voices through which the Word of God speaks to us today.

Richard Bauckham
University of Manchester

JUDE

INTRODUCTION

Author, place, and date

The "Jude" to whom the letter of Jude is ascribed is Judas the brother of Jesus (Mark 6:3). This is made quite clear by the phrase "brother of James" (v 1), which distinguishes this Judas from others of the same name by mentioning his relation to James the brother of the Lord, the only man in the early church who could be called simply "James" without risk of ambiguity. Many modern scholars have considered the letter pseudepigraphal, written by a later Christian who attributed his work to the brother of the Lord. But the arguments for this view (which cannot be discussed here) are exegetically weak. The general character of the letter, when properly understood, supports the view that it was written by Jude the Lord's brother himself.[1]

Jude was one of the four (half- or step-) brothers of Jesus (Mark 6:3), but we know much less about him than about his elder brother James. From 1 Corinthians 9:5 and some other evidence in early Christian literature, it seems that, whereas

James remained resident in Jerusalem and became the leader of the church there, the other brothers of Jesus were traveling missionaries, preaching the gospel throughout Palestine and perhaps also elsewhere.[2] We do not know who the readers to whom Jude's letter was first addressed were, except that they were most probably Jewish Christians. But since the problem of false teaching which occasioned the letter is a particular one, the letter was certainly addressed to a specific church or group of churches. The letter contains no secure indication of date: it could well date from the fifties A.D. and be one of the earliest of the New Testament documents, or it could have been written rather later, toward the end of Jude's missionary career.

The special interest of the letter of Jude is that it is one of the very few surviving documents of early Palestinian Jewish Christianity—the original Christian movement from which the whole of the rest of the early Christian movement derived. It offers us a glimpse of the convictions about Jesus and the Gospel which were preached by the earliest Jewish Christian missionaries in Palestine.

The opponents

In verses 3 and 4 Jude explains that his letter is not the extended discussion of Christian salvation he had intended to write, but a more ad hoc response to the news that the churches have been infiltrated by a group of itinerant teachers whose lifestyle and message he considers dangerous to his readers. To appreciate Jude's message today, we need some understanding of the character of these opponents, with whom his letter is preoccupied. Although they have often been identified as Gnostics, there is no clear evidence of Gnostic teaching in what Jude says about them. What is clear is that they were antinomians, who took Christian freedom to mean freedom from all moral constraint. They seem to have been itinerant prophets, like many of those who traveled around the early Christian churches. They were accepted at the church's fellowship meals (v 12a), where they laid claim to charismatic inspiration, manifested in visions (v 8: "dreamings") through which they received their antinomian teachings.

On the strength of this charismatic authority of their own, they disparaged the angels who were regarded as the guardians of the moral order (v 8b) and evidently regarded themselves and their followers as the truly spiritual people, distinguished from more conventional Christians by their Spirit-inspired freedom from all external authority (cf. v 19). It is possible, but not certain, that this charismatic antinomianism represents a distortion of Paul's teaching about Christian freedom from the law. In any case, Jude sees in it a rejection of the authority of the Lord Jesus (vv 4, 8). Against it, his letter insists on the necessary moral implications of the Christian gospel.

The structure of the letter

Many misunderstandings of the letter of Jude have arisen from a failure to appreciate its literary structure. The general structure of the letter can be analyzed as follows:

Analysis of the Letter

Address and greeting (1–2)

Occasion and theme of the letter (3–4)

    A. The appeal to contend for the faith (3)

    B. The background to the appeal: the false teachers, their character and judgment (4)

       (forming introductory statement of theme for B^1)

Body of the letter (5–23)

    B^1. The background: a commentary on four prophecies of the doom of the ungodly (5–19)

A¹. The appeal (20-23)

    (i)   Four exhortations on Christian living (20-21)

    (ii) Advice on dealing with offenders (22-23)

Concluding doxology. (24-25)

In this analysis it should be noted especially that the initial statement of the theme of the letter (vv 3-4) contains two parts (here labeled A and B) which correspond, in reverse order, to the two parts of the body of the letter (labeled B¹ and A¹). The main purpose of the letter is the appeal "to contend for the faith" which is announced in verse 3 and spelled out in verses 20-23.

But verse 4 explains that this appeal is necessary because the readers are in danger of being misled by false teachers. The claim in verse 4 that these teachers are people whose ungodly behavior has already been condemned by God is then substantiated by the exegetical section (vv 5-19), which argues that these are the people to whom the scriptural types and prophecies of judgment refer. Thus we should not be misled by the length and central position of the discussion of the false teachers (vv 4-19) into considering it the main object of the letter. This section establishes the danger in which the readers are placed by the influence of the false teachers. So it performs an essential role as background to the appeal, but the real climax of the letter is only reached in the exhortations of verses 20-23.

In verses 4-19 Jude establishes the need for his readers to "contend for the faith," but only in verses 20-23 does he explain what "contending for the faith" involves. Thus his negative polemic against the false teachers is subordinate to the positive Christian teaching of verses 20-23, where he combines awareness of the danger of the false teachers' influence with a pastoral concern for their reclamation. He then concludes with a truly magnificent doxology (vv 24-25), which is, in effect, a confident prayer that God will preserve the readers from spiritual disaster and achieve his eschatological purpose for them.

Jude's exegesis

The form of the exegetical section (B¹: vv 5–19) requires further explanation. Together with its introductory statement of theme (B: v 4), it can be analyzed as follows:

Analysis of the Commentary Section

Introductory statement of theme	4
"Text" 1: Three Old Testament types	5–7
and interpretation	8–10
including secondary "text" 1a: Michael and the devil	9
"Text" 2: Three more Old Testament types	11
and interpretation	12–13
including secondary allusions (Ezek 34:2; Prov 25:14; Isa 57:20; 1 Enoch 80:6)	12–13
"Text" 3: A very ancient prophecy (1 Enoch 1:9)	14–15
and interpretation	16
"Text" 4: A very modern prophecy (a prophecy of the apostles)	17–18
and interpretation	19

This section is not, as it might at first seem to a modern reader, mere undisciplined denunciation. It is a very carefully composed piece of scriptural commentary (in my commentary on Jude, I called it a *"midrash"**) which argues for the statement made in verse 4: that the false teachers are people whose condemnation has long been prophesied. It does this by showing that the libertine teaching and behavior of the false teachers corresponds to that of the ungodly people of the last days, whose judgment at the coming of the Lord is foretold in scriptural types and prophecies. Both the assumption that Scripture is prophetic of the last times in which the author and his readers are living, and the

---

* Midrash is the Jewish term for a commentary on Scripture.

exegetical methods used to apply Scripture to the present, resemble ancient Jewish types of scriptural commentary such as those found among the Dead Sea Scrolls.

Jude cites a series of four main "texts" (vv 5–7, 11, 14–15, 17–18) and comments on each (vv 8–10, 12–13, 16, 19). The "texts" are not always actual quotations. The first two are summary references to Old Testament figures who are taken to be types of the ungodly of the last days. The third is a prophecy quoted from the apocryphal apocalypse of Enoch (1 Enoch 1:9), while the fourth refers to predictions of the apostles, summarized in the author's own words.

The passages of commentary contain further allusions to Scripture, introduced to help the exposition of the main "texts." The most prominent of these is the reference to an apocryphal account of the burial of Moses in verse 9. But in each case the transition from "text" to commentary is clearly marked by a reference to "these" or "these men," which indicates that Jude's opponents ("these") are the people to whom the "text" refers, and by a transition from the past or the future tense to the present tense, indicating that the type or prophecy is now being fulfilled in the present. Another feature of the exegetical method is the use of catchwords to link the "text" with the commentary and to link "texts" together. These are usually lost in English translation, but an example which survives in the RSV is "revile" in verses 8–10.

We have to appreciate that in this commentary section Jude is engaging, in a very learned and skillful way, in the kind of scriptural exegesis which contemporary Jewish exegetes practiced. The result is sometimes strange to us, but it belongs to the attempt of the earliest Jewish Christians to understand and explain their faith within their own religious culture. Many modern readers have been especially puzzled by Jude's use of apocryphal literature. He evidently had great respect for the Jewish apocalyptic work we know as 1 Enoch, which he not only quotes explicitly in verses 14-15, but also echoes elsewhere, especially in verses 6, 12-13. The reference in verse 9 is to an apocryphal text no longer extant, though it may have been the lost ending of the Testament of Moses.³ Precisely what status, in relation to the canonical Scriptures of the Hebrew Bible, Jude gave to these apocryphal works, we cannot tell. We need not suppose that he included them in his canon of Scripture, especially since his quotation from 1 Enoch (vv 14-15) is paired with a clearly nonscriptural prophecy, an oral prophecy of the apostles (v 18). But these apocryphal works must have been valued in the circles to which Jude belonged.

Themes

Despite its brevity, the letter of Jude is quite rich in content, owing to its masterly composition and its remarkable economy of expression, which at times achieves an almost poetic effect. Its major themes are all closely connected with the specific aim of the letter: to warn the readers against the danger of the antinomian teaching of the opponents and to advise them on their response to this dangerous situation. For convenience we can identify three major topics: morality and judgment, Christian living, and the Lordship of Jesus Christ.

1 MORALITY AND JUDGMENT

Jude is not engaged in a purely doctrinal controversy about matters such as the nature of God or the divinity of Christ. His concern is not so much with orthodoxy as with orthopraxy. His point of difference with his opponents concerns the moral implications of the gospel. In common with all the New Testament writers, he holds that faith in Jesus Christ entails a corresponding way of life. Those who acknowledge Jesus as Lord must live in obedience to him. Jude therefore perceives his opponents to be a serious danger to the faith and the salvation of his readers because they deny the moral implications of the gospel. They are antinomians, i.e., people who not only neglect the moral commandments in practice, but reject them in principle and teach others to do so too. In this attack on the moral implications of the gospel, Jude sees that the gospel itself ("the faith," v 3) is at stake, since God's purpose in the gospel is to save sinners, not to promote sin. In order to highlight the moral seriousness of Christian faith, Jude insists on the reality of divine judgment for those who deliberately flout the moral authority of the Lord and teach others to do so.

The opponents

As we have noted in the introduction, Jude puts his condemnation of his opponents into the form of a scriptural commentary (vv 5-19), of which verse 4 is the opening statement of theme. The commentary is designed to show that the character of the opponents, as people who practice and teach immorality, identifies them as people whose judgment has been prophesied. We shall first of all gather the information Jude supplies as to the character of the opponents, before turning to his conviction of their coming judgment.

The opponents are first described by the single, potent word "ungodly" (v 4: Greek *asebeis*). This is a catchword which Jude picks up again later (vv 15, 18). His brief letter in fact contains six occurrences of words belonging to the word group *aseb-*, more than any other New Testament writing. Four of these occur in the quotation from Enoch (vv 14-15), which Jude surely selected partly because its repetitive use of these words emphasizes the ungodliness of those who are to be condemned at the judgment. Although the basic meaning of the *aseb-* words in Greek is irreverence to the gods or God, in Jewish usage, which provides the background for Jude's use, they had a strong ethical sense. Because, for the Jew, God's commandments regulate the whole of human life, an irreverent attitude to God is shown in unrighteous conduct. For Jude this word aptly sums up the antinomianism of the false teachers: unrighteous behavior stemming from an irreverent rejection of the authority of God's commandments.

These ungodly people "pervert the grace of God into immorality." The Christian gospel proclaimed God's free grace or favor to sinners, delivering them from condemnation and sin. Properly understood, this meant that sinners were set free to live righteously. But there is a good deal of evidence for an antinomian misinterpretation of Christian freedom in some early Christian circles (1 Cor 5:1-6; 6:12-20; 10:23; 2 Pet 2:19; Rev 2:14, 20; cf., the danger suggested in Rom 3:8; 6:1,15; Gal 5:13; 1 Pet 2:16).

Jude's opponents took this line, interpreting the Christian's liberation by God's grace as a liberation from all moral constraint. In this way they perverted the purpose of God's grace—which is to make sinners righteous—into a justification of immorality. The additional statement in verse 4 that they "deny our only Sovereign and Lord Jesus Christ" does not mean that they were guilty of christological heresy. Rather, it is by rejecting his moral demands that they in effect deny him. They repudiate his Lordship—a point which Jude takes up again in verse 8.

Old Testament comparisons

In verses 5-13 Jude compares his opponents with well-known examples of sin and judgment from the Old Testament. The material is carefully structured. The first set of three Old Testament examples (vv 5-7), with the application of them to Jude's opponents (vv 8-10), characterizes the opponents as people who practice flagrant immorality, while the second set of three Old Testament figures (v 11), with its exposition (vv 12-13), characterizes them as people who teach others to behave immorally.

If we look closely at the three examples of sin in verses 5-7, we shall see that two main points are made. One point links the first and second examples; the other links the second and third. The faithless generation of Israel in the wilderness (Jude is thinking of Numbers 14; cf. Deut 1:32; 9:23; Ps 106:24-25) and the fallen angels are examples of apostasy. Israel was the Lord's own people, who had experienced his liberating grace in the Exodus, but went on to

Morality and Judgment

reject his authority over them. The angels are "the sons of God" of Genesis 6:1-4, as interpreted in Jewish tradition (v 6 alludes specifically to passages in the account of them in 1 Enoch 6-11). They left their position of heavenly power, which they had exercised in the service of God, in order to subvert God's purpose on earth. The false teachers resemble both groups in that having once accepted the authority of the Lord, they now reject it (v 8).

But a common theme also links the sin of the angels with that of the inhabitants of Sodom and Gomorrah, who are said to have "practiced immorality in the same way as the angels" (v 7). The point here is that, in Jewish tradition, the initial sin of the angels was their sexual desire for and union with women. The corresponding sin of the Sodomites was not, in this instance, homosexual desire, but their desire for sexual relations with angels (Gen 19:4-11). The two cases had already been compared in Jewish tradition, as examples of outrageous transgression of the order of creation.

By picking out these extreme—even bizarre—examples, Jude wishes to characterize immorality as violation of the created order of the world. The opponents are doubtless not guilty of this particular sexual perversion, but their sexual misconduct (they "defile the flesh," v 8) is a deliberate rejection of the divinely ordained order of things. We are reminded that Christian obedience to Christ is not a matter of a new and different morality, replacing the order of creation, but precisely a restoration and fulfillment of God's moral purpose in creation. Christian living consists not in flouting, but in fulfilling, the moral order of creation.

The three Old Testament figures in verse 11 have to be understood in the light of their portrayal in Jewish exegetical tradition in Jude's time. In this light their common characteristic is that they led others into sin. Cain was not simply the first murderer, but the archetypal sinner who corrupted the whole race of Adam. Balaam was the prophet who, in his greed for financial gain, hurried eagerly to advise Balak to entice Israel into sin and so brought about the apostasy of Israel at Beth-peor (Num 25:1-3; cf., 31:16). Korah, who contested the authority of Moses and was said to have disputed the divine origin of certain laws, gathering followers around him, had become the archetypal antinomian teacher. It is therefore as teachers of immorality that the opponents are said to be following in the footsteps of these three.

The series of metaphors in verses 12-13 reinforce the point. Of special interest are the four metaphors from nature, one from each region of the universe (clouds in the air, trees on the earth, waves of the sea, stars in the heavens). Each of these portrays the opponents precisely as teachers— clouds and rain which promise benefits but fail to deliver them, trees which produce no fruit, waves which corrupt what they touch, stars which go astray from their courses and so mislead those who look to them for guidance. Furthermore, each is also an example of nature failing to fulfill the laws ordained for her. In this lawlessness of nature, Jude sees an image of the lawlessness of his opponents. Once again the sense of an order of creation, which these people are transgressing and teaching others to transgress, lies in the background.

Spiritual pride

One final point about the opponents can be gathered from verses 8, 10, and 19. They claimed prophetic inspiration in visions ("dreamings," v 8), and they gathered around them an elitist group of other people who similarly claimed to possess the Spirit (hence they "create divisions," v 19). Evidently, their antinomianism was rooted in spiritual *pride*. They were the people who *really* possessed the Spirit, and in this consciousness of spiritual elevation they felt themselves liberated from the moral constraints with which unspiritual people are burdened. The order of creation no longer bound them, for they were spiritual people. They expressed their new being, their sense of moral autonomy, in expressions of contempt for the angels who acted as guardians of the moral order of creation (v 8).

But Jude has a keen sense of the irony of this claim to spiritual superiority. In fact, they are not spiritual (*pneumatikos*), possessing the Spirit, but natural, earthly, unspiritual (*psychikos*; v 19) people, who follow their own natural instincts, "their own desires for ungodliness" (v 18). Their indulgence of the flesh (v 8) shows this. In their pretended knowledge of the spiritual world, they "slander whatever they do not understand" (the angels), while at the same time their behavior shows that what they understand only too well are their sexual drives. These people who claim to be spiritual, superior to the angels, prove themselves to be living only on the subhuman level of the beasts (v 10).

Jude's exposure of these spiritual impostors is a warning against every tendency to a pseudospirituality in which people claim to be liberated or raised above that created order which is subject to the moral authority of God. Those who try to exceed their human place in creation usually plunge below it. But those who truly possess the Spirit live under the Lordship of Christ, which is the fulfillment of the moral order of creation and the restoration of the properly human place in creation.

Judgment

Jude's Old Testament examples are examples not only of sin, but also of judgment. They were among the best-known examples of divine judgment in history. But they were more than that. Like many Jews and early Christians, Jude read the Old Testament history as pointing forward to the last days and the consummation of history. The way that God has already acted in history, in salvation, and judgment provides the model for the way he will finally fulfill his purpose for history, in eschatological salvation and judgment. God's end-time action will, of course, surpass his acts in history, but it will also correspond to them.

New Testament typology can therefore be appropriately described as eschatological typology: God's acts in the Old Testament history are types which point forward to, and are surpassed by, his final acts in Christ. Thus Jude's examples of divine judgment are not just examples. They are types which point forward to the judgment of the last day, at which the Lord Jesus will exercise the judgment which belongs to his eschatological saving work. They are in a sense *prophecies* of the judgment on the sinners of the last times.

We can therefore understand that Jude follows his two sets of Old Testament types with two actual prophecies. One, ascribed to Enoch, describes the eschatological coming of the Lord to judge the ungodly (vv 14–15). The other is a summary of the prophetic teaching of the apostles, who commonly warned newly established Christian communities about the ungodly people of the last times, in which they were living (v 18). Although the quotation does not explicitly say that these ungodly people will incur judgment at the Lord's coming, this threat is to be understood.

Jude's argument is that because his opponents conform to these types and prophecies of ungodly people, they will incur the prophesied judgment on such people. It should be noted carefully that this identification of his opponents as figures of prophecy is not fatalistic, but *functional*. In other words, by their behavior these people identify themselves with the doomed ungodly of prophecy. The ungodly whose fate at the judgment is prophesied are, so to speak, an open category into which any who behave like that put themselves. They can also remove themselves from that category by repentance; Jude has not given up on his opponents, as verses 22-23 will show us later. But verses 4-19 are not addressed to the opponents themselves, as a call to repentance. They are addressed to Jude's readers, as a warning of the danger in which their opponents place them: the danger of incurring the judgment which behavior like that of the opponents incurs.

Jude, like most New Testament writers, writes as though the coming of Christ to eschatological judgment—the Parousia, the énd of history—will occur within the lifetime of his contemporaries. This should be no great problem to us. At a superficially literal level, this common early Christian assumption was a mistake. But at a profounder, theological level it expressed an important truth. Whether or not we shall survive to the judgment, we must all live in the light of it. What will be exposed when Jesus Christ brings God's purpose in history to its fulfillment is the final truth of all our lives. Those who have lived their lives deliberately counter to his purpose—who have known the way to righteousness but have made a deliberate choice to be sinners—must perish under that exposure. It cannot be otherwise if God is righteous, if he has made us so that we cannot fulfill ourselves except in righteousness, and if he has promised that righteousness, for the good of his whole creation, must in the end prevail.

2   CHRISTIAN LIVING

The condemnation of his opponents as ungodly people whose judgment has been prophesied is not the main point of Jude's letter. It is a point which very much needed to be made, in order to alert his readers to the danger they were in. But it was subsidiary to the positive main point, which was to urge his readers to resist the influence of the false teachers and to continue to live faithful Christian lives in obedience to the gospel. To remind them of the central characteristics of faithful Christian living was Jude's unsensational, but necessary, aim in writing.

Contending for the Faith

Jude announces the purpose of his letter in verse 3: it is to appeal to his readers "to carry on the fight for the faith which was once and for all delivered to the saints." Here "the faith" is used in the sense of the content of what is believed. Much later than Jude the term came to imply a detailed statement of Christian beliefs such as we have in the creeds of the early church. But this is not Jude's meaning. He uses "the faith," as Paul sometimes does (e.g., Gal 1:23), to mean simply "the gospel," the central Christian message of salvation through Jesus Christ. In the situation to which he writes, it is not some particular point of orthodox belief that is at stake, but the gospel itself. The antinomian teaching of the opponents, by denying the moral implications of the gospel, is undermining the whole point of the gospel, which is to save sinners from sin and make them righteous.

Jude has two ways of enabling his readers to identify "the faith" correctly, in distinction from the perversion of the gospel taught by the opponents. In verse 3, he calls it "the faith which was once and for all delivered to the saints"; in verse 20, he calls it "your most holy faith."

The first of these descriptions recalls the readers to the original missionary preaching of the apostles who founded their church(es). In that first preaching of the gospel in that area, the apostles handed on to their first converts ("the saints") the authentic Christian message ("the faith") as they themselves had received it from their Lord. They handed it on "once and for all" because it is the message of the "once and for all" salvific action of God in the history of Jesus Christ (Rom 6:10; Heb 9:12, 26–28; 10:10; 1 Pet 3:18). So the essential Christian message cannot change. Of course, this does not imply a rigid adherence to a particular formulation of the gospel. The way the gospel needs to be expressed, and its implications in different contexts, may need to change: in the various New Testament writings themselves we see different ways of expressing and drawing out the implications of the gospel. But the essential message itself is given once and for all. This is why early Christian teachers, like Jude and Paul (Rom 16:17; 2 Cor 11:4; Gal 1:9), referred their readers back to the gospel as it was first received by those churches from their founding apostles as the standard by which all subsequent teaching was to be tested and false teaching exposed. For the same reason, the scriptural record of the apostolic gospel in the New Testament must serve as the standard and test of all Christian teaching for us.

. In calling the gospel *"your* most holy faith" (v 20), Jude again implies that it is the gospel his readers have received and believed, as distinct from the false gospel now being introduced by his opponents. It is "most holy" because it comes from the holy God and makes its recipients holy. It makes them "the saints" (holy ones, v 3), a people who belong to God and must therefore live lives obedient to him, reflecting his righteousness (cf., 1 Pet 1:14–16). In this way Jude indicates that the moral implications of the gospel are integral to its very nature. The antinomianism of the false teachers amounts to another gospel.

So how does Jude expect his readers "to carry on the fight for the faith" (v 3)? He does not ask them to *start* fighting on behalf of the gospel, as though the fight only begins now that the gospel is threatened by the false teachers. The Greek word he uses (*epagōnizesthai*) probably indicates that they are to continue a fight in which they are already engaged. The false teachers and their message are not the enemy against whom they fight (the metaphor of fighting, taken from the Greek games, need not imply an enemy at all). It is not a case of *defending* the gospel against attacks. Rather, Jude's readers are in danger of being deflected from their fight by the false teachers and their message; so that Jude has to urge them not to listen to the false teachers, but to carry on the fight in which they were already engaged before the false teachers arrived. The fight which Jude has in mind is that which Christians carry on by being faithful to the gospel in their lives, by living out the gospel in the life of the church (cf., Phil 1:27). The struggle of Christian living is a contest on behalf of the gospel, not in the sense of merely *defending* the gospel against attacks, but in the offensive sense of positively promoting the advance and victory of the gospel in human life. The false teachers are a threat to Jude's readers because they are persuading them not to live out the gospel in their lives, in effect to give up contending for the faith.

It becomes clear, as we have already seen in the introduction with reference to the structure of Jude's letter, that Jude's notion of contending for the faith is not spelled out in verses 4–19, but in verses 20–23. In verses 4–19 he is alerting his readers to the danger which makes it necessary for him to appeal to them to go on contending for the faith. The appeal itself consists of the positive exhortations to faithful Christian living which appear in verses 20–21, along with the pastoral advice on dealing with the false teachers and their disciples in verses 22–23. These verses (20–23) are not, as they have so often been treated, an appendix of secondary importance, but the climax of Jude's letter.

Four essentials of Christian living

Jude provides his readers with a masterly succinct summary of what it means to live in faithfulness to the gospel (vv 20–21). These four commands are doubtless not original but drawn from traditional forms of Christian teaching. After all, Jude intended nothing new. He wrote to recall his readers to what they had known since the time of their instruction as new Christians. If they are to resist the false teaching, they must simply go on living as they already know Christians should live. This is always the most important response to teaching which threatens the integrity of Christian discipleship.

But if the commands are not new, Jude has carefully selected this set of four. That the four commands encompass the whole of Christian life is indicated by the fact that they incorporate two patterns of three which were very familiar in early Christian teaching. The second, third, and fourth of Jude's injunctions refer respectively to the three persons

of the Trinity—the Holy Spirit, God, Jesus Christ—
indicating that the way of life demanded is a response in
faith to the trinitarian God as he is known in the gospel.
The first, third, and fourth injunctions represent the familiar triad of faith, love, and hope—a way of summarizing
what is involved in living according to the gospel, which
Paul also took over from early tradition.

The first command is to "build yourselves up on the
foundation of your most holy faith." It evokes the image of
the Christian community as a building—the eschatological
temple of God—of which the gospel is the foundation. (Paul
in a different, though not contradictory, use of this image
regards Jesus Christ himself as the foundation, 1 Cor 3:11.)
The meaning is not that each of Jude's readers should build
himself or herself up, but that all should contribute to the
spiritual growth of the whole community. If they build on
the foundation of their *holy* faith, then the community they
build will be a holy one, living out the moral requirements of
the gospel.

The second command is to pray with the inspiration of the
Holy Spirit. The opponents falsely claimed the inspiration of
the Spirit. It is perhaps significant that in contrast to the
visions and prophecies which the opponents put forward as
the effects of their possession of the Spirit, Jude makes *prayer*
in the Spirit one of his four essentials of Christian living.
Visions and prophecies may be important to the life of the
church, but Spirit-inspired prayer is essential to the life of
the church and to the life of each and every Christian. The
opponents misunderstood the Spirit as raising them above
the life of creaturely obedience to God. Their visions and
prophecies fed this spiritual conceit. Prayer is less open to
such distortion. It makes us aware of our dependence on
God. Prayer inspired by the Spirit of Christ expresses our
relation to God as our Father, on whom we are wholly dependent and to whom we owe absolute obedience.

The third command, to "keep yourselves in the love of God," can be well expounded by a Johannine parallel (though it refers to remaining in Christ's love, rather than God's): "Now remain in my love. If you obey my commands, you will remain in my love, just as I have obeyed my Father's commands and remain in his love" (John 15:9b-10). It is not that God's love for us is conditional, but that we can exclude ourselves from it if we do not respond to it by living as he demands of us.

Finally, the fourth command characterizes Christian living as living toward its eschatological goal. The idea of "waiting," which is frequently used in early Christian literature to describe the orientation of Christian life toward the Parousia, is not intended to suggest a purely passive attitude. It describes the way in which the whole existence of the early Christians was lived in the light of the coming Parousia, when the truth of all human lives will be exposed under God's judgment. It means living in readiness for that day. It means living all the time as we would want the Lord Jesus to find us when he comes.

Jude has made it more than plain that those who live ungodly lives, deliberately flouting God's saving intention in Christ, can expect only condemnation at the judgment. But those who live out the gospel in their lives can expect "the mercy of our Lord Jesus Christ to eternal life" (v 21). We should note carefully that it is mercy they expect. Their faithful Christian lives do not entitle them to eternal life as a right. Only as forgiven sinners can they receive eternal life through God's mercy. What distinguishes them from the ungodly is that they take their forgiveness seriously.

Dealing with those who err

The manuscript evidence for verses 22-23 constitutes one of the most confused textual situations in the New

Testament, and it is impossible to be sure what the original text was. In my commentary I argued that the most probable original text is that of the oldest extant manuscript (P^{72}), which should be translated:

Snatch some from the fire,
but on those who dispute have mercy with fear,
hating even the clothing that has been soiled by the
flesh.

Jude's language here is strongly influenced by Zechariah 3:2–4, which accounts for the metaphors he uses. What would otherwise be rather obscure instructions would not have been for his first readers, because he takes for granted their familiarity with the usual early Christian procedures for dealing with those guilty of serious sin and propagators of dangerously false teaching. He assumes that his readers, in a spirit of Christian love, are going to warn the false teachers and their disciples of the danger of judgment they are incurring and call them to repentance.

The first of his two instructions refers to those with whom this approach is successful. By warning and restoring the sinners, Jude's readers will "snatch some from the fire." The metaphor (taken from Zech 3:2, but given new meaning) envisages the sinners as poised on the brink of hell-fire and saved at the last moment from plunging into it. We see both the seriousness with which Jude takes the threat of imminent judgment hanging over his opponents and also that he is far from content to leave them to their fate. The extremity of their danger arouses his pastoral concern to save them from it.

He also anticipates, however, that some will not respond to their fellow-Christians' loving rebuke, but "dispute" (i.e., argue against it) continuing to assert their antinomian teaching in self-justification. But not even these are to be abandoned to their fate; far from it. Jude's readers must continue to "have mercy" on them, to seek their salvation by prayer and whatever other means might be available. But Jude is also very conscious of the danger which these unrepentant teachers of error constitute for his readers. His advice is to "have mercy *with fear,*" i.e., taking the greatest possible care to avoid being influenced by them. His readers must fear the judgment of God, which they too will incur if they are infected by the sins of these sinners. Just as earlier he had compared the false teachers with rocks, close contact with which causes shipwreck (v 12: "dangerous reefs"), so now he uses the metaphor (taken from Zech 3:3–4) of clothes soiled by the body's excretions to suggest the contaminating effect of their sin on everything around them. Probably he means that personal contact with the false teachers should normally be avoided (cf., 2 John 10–11) for fear of their influence.

In these instructions we see Jude as a true Christian pastor in a serious situation. His pastoral concern embraces both his readers, who need to be protected from the dangerous influence of the false teachers, and the false teachers themselves, and those who have already been won over by them. Despite their apostasy, the latter are no less than the former the object of his continuing love. The strong emphasis on judgment in his letter has not hardened his heart against them. It has awakened his pastoral concern for them. He combines abhorrence for the sins they are promoting, firm belief in God's judgment on sin, with a genuinely Christian desire for the reclamation of even the most obstinate.

The goal of Christian living

The words of verse 21, "keep yourselves in the love of God," might suggest that it lies solely within the power and responsibility of Jude's readers to remain faithful and attain the goal of salvation: eternal life. This power and responsibility are certainly real and needed to be stressed against the antinomianism of the false teachers. But they are only one side of the coin, as Jude himself makes quite clear. Jude's deliberate literary technique of making catchword connections between parts of his letter links these words of verse 21 ("keep yourselves in the love of God") with his opening description of his readers in verse 1: "loved in God the Father and kept for Jesus Christ."

Jude is confident that his readers are *kept safe by God* for the Parousia of Jesus Christ, when they will enter into their final salvation. Because they belong to Jesus their Lord, God keeps them safe for him until he comes to claim them as his own. Thus the readers' own responsibility to keep themselves within the love of God is enclosed within God's loving keeping of them. The mystery of human responsibility within the divine sovereignty is not, however, explained by Jude. His point is not a theoretical but an existential one: Christians can exercise their real responsibility to remain faithful to God within a sustaining assurance of God's power to keep them in his love.

Jude returns to this point in his magnificent concluding doxology (vv 24–25), which is not only an ascription of praise to God but also a confident prayer that God will preserve his readers from the spiritual disaster with which the false teaching threatens them and bring them to the eschatological destiny he intends for them. This destiny is portrayed in the words: "to present you without blemish in the presence of his glory, with rejoicing" (v 24). Jude here pictures the last day as the eschatological festival of worship, in which the achievement of God's purposes for his people will take the form of his presentation of them as perfect sacrifices in the heavenly sanctuary, offered up to the glory of God amid the jubilation of the worshipers. This, in the end, is the purpose of Christian living. All Jude's concerns in his letter, to combat the false teaching for the sake of the health of the church and the Christian obedience of its members, are finally aimed at this goal: that they should in the end be found fit to be a sacrificial offering to God.

3   JESUS THE LORD

In the short letter of Jude we cannot expect to find a complete Christology. He did not write for that purpose. But there is enough relevant material in it to give us important insight into the way Jesus was regarded in the Palestinian Jewish Christian movement of which Jude was a leader [1]

Jesus the Messiah

Jude never uses simply the personal name Jesus; nor does he ever use the title Christ (Messiah) without the name Jesus. He always uses the two in combination: Jesus Christ (vv 1, 4, 17, 21, 25). Already, in the Jewish Christianity of Palestine, "the Messiah" was on the way to becoming a kind of surname for Jesus. But this was certainly not because the meaning of the designation Messiah was being forgotten, as though it were becoming a *mere* name without meaning. Rather it was because Christians needed a way of distinguishing their Jesus from others who bore this very common name. They could, and sometimes did, call him "Jesus of Nazareth," as non-Christian Jews did, but they preferred "Jesus the Messiah" because it distinguished Jesus in the way that was theologically decisive for them. It indicated not only which Jesus it was that they preached but also why they preached him. That God had anointed Jesus as his Messiah was the fundamental theological fact about Jesus which made them Christians and gave them their gospel. The belief that Jesus was the Messiah was what distinguished Christian Jews from other Jews. So fundamental was this designation of Jesus that it spread from the earliest Palestinian church to all other branches of early Christianity and gave Christians the name by which they became universally known.

For the first Christians, Jesus' messiahship meant that he was the descendant of David whom God had anointed as his eschatological viceroy, the one who was accomplishing God's final purpose in history, the agent of final salvation and judgment. It indicated the uniqueness and finality of Jesus' role in the divine purpose; and it suggested that, as God's vicegerent, he exercises God's authority to save and to judge. However, it is noteworthy that Jude is content to call Jesus "Jesus the Messiah" (Jesus Christ) only in the opening address and greeting of his letter (v 1, twice). Once he moves into the body of his letter he always combines "Jesus Christ" with "our Lord" (vv 4, 17, 21, 25). This is because he is not content to leave the implication of Jesus' divine authority implicit, as it is in the designation Messiah; he wishes to make it explicit, as it is in the title Lord.

The title "Lord"

Jude's emphasis on the Lordship of Jesus is characteristic of early Christianity generally, but in his case it should also be connected with his polemic against the false teachers. Their error was precisely to repudiate the moral authority of

Jesus as the Lord of his people and as the coming Judge of the world. Hence Jude's first reference to Jesus' Lordship is in his summary statement of the error and danger of the false teachers (v 4), and takes the emphatic form: "our only Sovereign and Lord." Here Jude uses not only the word which early Christians very commonly used to designate Jesus as "Lord" (*kyrios*), but also a word meaning "Master" or "Sovereign" (*despotēs*), which was very rarely used of Jesus. To this combination of titles we shall return.

After verse 4 Jude three times calls Jesus "our Lord" (vv 17, 21: "our Lord Jesus Christ"; v 25: "Jesus Christ our Lord"). He also calls Jesus "the Lord" in verse 14 (we shall discuss this usage shortly). In verse 9, however, "the Lord" is probably God rather than Jesus.

More problematic is verse 5, where the majority of manuscripts read "the Lord who saved a people out of the land of Egypt . . . ," but some important textual authorities have "Jesus who saved a people out of the land of Egypt. . . ." Some scholars accept the reading "Jesus"; others prefer "the Lord" and understand it to refer to Jesus; others also prefer the reading "the Lord" but interpret it as a reference to God. I have argued elsewhere for this last position.[2] Jude is not in verse 5 referring explicitly to the preexistent Christ, but he is referring to the same divine Lordship which is now exercised by Jesus Christ. The divine judgments of verses 5–7 are cited by Jude as types of the last judgment which will be carried out by the Lord Jesus. So the fact that the reference of "the Lord" varies in verses 5, 9, and 14 between God and Christ is natural. Jude is concerned throughout with that divine authority to judge which God has now delegated to his Messiah Jesus. It is this authority (*kyriotēs*) which his opponents reject (v 8) when they "deny our only Sovereign and Lord Jesus Christ" (v 4).

It has often been said that in the earliest Jewish Christianity, Jesus was called Lord primarily with reference to his future (and imminent) coming as Savior and Judge. The Aramaic invocation from the earliest churches, which has been preserved in Greek transliteration as "Maranatha" (1 Cor 16:22; Didache 10:6) and which should probably be understood to mean "Our Lord, come!" (*mārānā> >āthā>*), certainly points in that direction. But it also shows that the coming Lord can already be addressed as Lord in the present. Moreover, he is addressed as "*our* Lord." In other words, he has already gathered a community who now acknowledge him as their Lord, while awaiting his coming to complete their salvation.

It is doubtful if there was ever a Christology in which the Lordship of Christ did not evoke his constitution of the Christian community (through his ministry, death, and outpouring of the Spirit) and his present status as Lord (through his resurrection and exaltation by God) as well as his future coming as eschatological Savior and Judge. Jude has no occasion to refer to Christ's already accomplished work of salvation—except typologically in verse 5, which implies that the new people of God have been saved through a new exodus. But in calling Jesus "our Lord" he takes for granted the work of salvation which has made Jesus Lord of his people, the Christian community. Jude's focus, owing to the aim of his letter, is on the present Lordship of Jesus over his people, who owe him obedience as Lord now, and on his future coming to judge those who reject his Lordship (vv 14–15) and to complete the salvation of those who acknowledge that Lordship (v 21).

The Lord's coming to judgment (v 14)

In verses 14–15 Jude quotes an apocryphal prophecy of Enoch which begins, "Behold, the Lord came with his ten thousands of holy ones, to execute judgment on all. . . ." In its original context (1 Enoch 1:9) this is a prophecy of the eschatological coming of God to judge the wicked. The passage in 1 Enoch is based on a series of Old Testament texts about "the day of the Lord" (especially Deut 33:2; Isa 40:4, 10; Jer 25:31; Mic 1:3-4; and Hab 3:3-9), which were understood in Jewish apocalyptic writings as prophecies of the coming of God at the end of the history of this age to judge the wicked, to save his people, and to establish his kingdom. But "the Lord" is not in the original text of 1 Enoch 1:9. The subject there is unstated, but it must be understood from 1:3-4 to be "the great Holy One," "the eternal God." Jude has supplied the subject, and in doing so has interpreted the prophecy as a reference to the Parousia of the Lord Jesus.

In doing so, Jude is following a practice which seems to go back to the earliest Christians' interpretation of the Old Testament, in which "day of the Lord" prophecies of the coming of God to judgment were applied to the Parousia of Jesus Christ as judge. For example, Zechariah 14:5b ("Then the Lord your God will come, and all the holy ones with him") lies behind several New Testament passages about the Parousia (Matt 16:27; 25:31; Mark 8:38; Luke 9:26; 1 Thess 3:13; 4:14; 2 Thess 1:7; Rev 19:14), while Isaiah 40:10 ("Behold the Lord God comes with might . . . behold, his reward is with him, and his recompense before him") is echoed with reference to the Parousia in Revelation 20:12. And 2 Thessalonians 1:7-8 is dependent on Isaiah 66:15-16 ("For behold, the Lord will come in fire . . . to render his anger in fury, and his rebuke with flames of fire . . .").

Similarly, the Old Testament phrase "the day of the Lord" itself was applied to the Parousia, with "the Lord" understood as Jesus (1 Thess 5:2; 2 Thess 2:2; 2 Pet 3:10; cf., 1 Cor 1:8; 5:5; 2 Cor 1:14). It should be noted that many of the Old Testament prophecies which were thus interpreted of the Parousia begin with the words, "Behold, the Lord will come . . ." (or similar). In adapting the quotation from 1 Enoch 1:9 to read, "Behold, the Lord came . . ." (i.e., "will come": The past tense is used, as often in the Old Testament prophets, to express the certainty of a future event), Jude was not only applying the prophecy to the coming of the Lord Jesus; he was also conforming it to the familiar form of words in such prophecies.

The most interesting point about this early Christian exegetical practice is the way the eschatological coming of *God* is interpreted as the eschatological coming of *Jesus*. In the Old Testament prophecies "the Lord" represents, in the Hebrew text, the divine name, the tetragrammaton (YHWH). In New Testament times Jews considered the name too sacred to pronounce. In reading the text aloud, they usually substituted a word meaning "Lord." In Hebrew this was 'adōnāy ("my Lord"). Some Greek-speaking Jews reading the Old Testament in Greek were beginning to use the word *kyrios* ("Lord") for this purpose: This is the word which New Testament quotations of the Old Testament regularly use as a substitute for the tetragrammaton. (It seems that this was a common, but not the universal practice, and that, for example, other Greek-speaking Jews were in the habit of substituting *despotēs* ["Master," "Sovereign"] for the tetragrammaton.) Thus, when early Christians applied Old Testament texts about the eschatological coming of "the Lord" to Jesus' Parousia, they were in effect transferring the *divine name* to him (as Phil 2:9–11 makes quite clear). This is what Jude is also doing in verse 14.

It is important to note that early Christians did not apply Old Testament texts about "the Lord" to Jesus indiscriminately. In most New Testament quotations from the Old Testament which use "the Lord" (*kyrios*) to represent the tetragrammaton, "the Lord" is not Jesus but God. There are examples, besides the "day of the Lord" prophecies, of the application of such texts to Jesus, but they represent an occasional, rather than a consistent, exegetical practice. It seems that the practice began with a quite specific class of texts—"day of the Lord" prophecies applied to the Parousia—and spread to a few other, but by no means to all, passages.

This observation gives us a most important insight into the way that Christians first perceived the *divine* Lordship of Jesus. They did not simply identify Jesus with God, as though everything the Old Testament said about God could be applied to Jesus; but they saw Jesus as the one who carries out God's eschatological purpose of salvation and judgment. Therefore the royal and judicial authority which Jesus as God's Messiah exercised was *God's* authority. In this way the christological title "Lord"—indicating Jesus' royal and judicial authority as God's anointed viceroy—coalesced with God's name "Lord" (representing the tetragrammaton), which indicated God's royal and judicial authority. As the one who exercises God's authority on the last day, the divine name in prophecies of the last day can refer to Jesus.

Jude's use of "the Lord" in verse 14 therefore carries a surprising amount of significance. It designates Jesus as the one whom God has appointed to carry out the whole of his eschatological purpose on his behalf, who therefore acts with God's authority to save and to judge, and who therefore bears the divine name itself. Though it does not simply identify Jesus with God, it strongly assimilates Jesus to God. The Lordship of God is Jesus' Lordship; and God is known now and in the future only through Jesus. The seeds of all later Christian thinking about Jesus' divinity can be found in this original Jewish-Christian understanding of Jesus as the one through whom all God's eschatological action occurs and therefore as the one to whom Christians address, in worship, their acknowledgment of the divine Lordship. It was only a matter of time before the one who was worshiped as Lord had to be explicitly understood as belonging to the being of God.

Our only Sovereign and Lord (v 4)

We have already noticed that this emphatic statement of Jesus' authority as Lord is deliberately placed at the outset of Jude's condemnation of the false teachers. In their flagrant immorality, they were denying Jesus' exclusive authority, as their Lord, to command and to judge, and subjecting themselves instead to other lords (cf., Matt 6:24; Rom 6:12–23; Gal 4:3, 8–9; 2 Pet 2:19). But there are two other points to notice about the phrase.

First, it reinforces a point we have already made: that Jesus' authority as Lord is *God's* authority exercised by Jesus. The word *despotēs* was normally used in Greek either for the master of a household, with absolute authority over his family and slaves, or for the ruler of a state, whose unlimited power over a people was thought of by analogy with the master of a household. Jews quite commonly used it of God, and this Jewish use was sometimes continued by Christians (Luke 2:29; Acts 4:24; Rev 6:10). Sometimes Jews used it as a Greek substitute for the tetragrammaton (YHWH). Most probably Jude uses it of the royal and judicial authority of Jesus (so that "Sovereign" is a better translation than "Master"),[3] not with any meaning distinct from that of "Lord" (*kyrios*), but simply to reinforce the meaning. But the whole phrase—"our only Sovereign and Lord"—would carry, to Jewish ears, a strong indication of divinity. It is the kind of phrase which Jews used to confess the exclusive Lordship of the one God of Israel and to refuse idolatrous allegiance to other lords.[4] For Jewish monotheists it was inconceivable that "our only Sovereign and Lord" could be other than God. That Jude can speak of "our only Sovereign and Lord Jesus Christ" is remarkable testimony to the extent to which he identified Jesus' Lordship with God's.

When Christians worship and serve Jesus as their only Lord, the only one to whom they owe absolute obedience, they are not infringing monotheism but expressing monotheism in its Christian form. Jesus' Lordship is not another Lordship alongside or in competition with God's; it is not even subordinate to God's. It *is* God's Lordship.

The second point of interest about the phrase is more purely historical. The word *despotēs* is hardly ever used of Jesus in extant Christian literature before the late second century. The only instance apart from Jude 4 is 2 Peter 2:1, whose author is dependent on Jude and has simply taken the usage over from Jude 4.

However, we do know, from the third-century writer Julius Africanus, that in Palestinian Jewish Christianity the relatives of Jesus, who continued to be Christian leaders in the Jewish-Christian churches down to at least the early second century, were known as *hoi desposynoi,* "the people who belong to the Sovereign."[5] The term would have meant virtually "the royal family," suggesting the special dignity which Jewish Christians often attributed to the relatives of Jesus because of their relationship to the Messiah Jesus. But the use of this term for the relatives of Jesus indicates that in Palestinian Jewish-Christian circles Jesus must have been called *ho despotēs.* Jude's use of this term for Jesus therefore reflects an unusual usage which helps to locate his letter firmly within the Palestinian Jewish-Christian circles where Jesus' brothers were leaders.

2 PETER

INTRODUCTION

Second Peter presents itself as a testament or farewell discourse of the apostle Peter, written in the form of a letter shortly before his death (1:14). Its object is to remind the readers of Peter's teaching and to defend this teaching against objections raised by certain false teachers.[1]

The structure of the letter

The structure of 2 Peter can be analyzed as follows:

Address and Greeting (1:1-2)

T^1 Theme: a summary of Peter's message (1:3-11)

T^2 Occasion: Peter's testament (1:12-15)

A^1 First apologetic section (1:16-21)

Two replies to objection 1: that the apostles based their preaching of the Parousia on invented myths (1:16-19)

Reply to objection 2: that Old Testament prophecies were merely the products of human minds (1:20-21)

T^3 Peter's prediction of false teachers (2:1–3a)

A^2 Second apologetic section (2:3b–10a)
       Reply to objection 3: that divine judgment never happens (2:3b–10a)

E^1 Denunciation of the false teachers (2:10b–22)

T^4 Peter's prediction of scoffers (3:1–4)
       (including objection 4: v 4)

A^3 Third apologetic section (3:5–10)
       Two replies to objection 4: that the expectation of the Parousia is
       disproved by its delay (3:5–10)

E^2 Exhortation to holy living (3:11–16)

       Conclusion (3:17–18).

In this analysis three types of passage are identified (apart
from the opening and concluding passages): those which
belong to the genre of testament (labeled T^1-T^4), those
which are apologetic in character (labeled A^1-A^3), and two
passages of an exhortatory nature (E^1, E^2).

Second Peter is clearly a letter (1:1–2) written to churches
to which 1 Peter was addressed (3:1). But it also belongs to
the literary genre of "testament," which was well known
in the Jewish literature of the period. In such testaments an
Old Testament figure, such as Moses or Ezra, knowing that
his death is approaching, gives a final message to his people,
which typically includes ethical exhortation and prophetic
revelations of the future.

The genre had definite thematic and formal characteristics. In 2 Peter, four passages (T^1-T^4 in the analysis) particu-
larly resemble the Jewish testament literature and clearly
identify the work as Peter's testament. In 1:12–15, a passage
full of conventional testament language, Peter describes the
occasion for writing as his awareness of approaching death
and his desire to provide for his teaching to be remembered
after his death. This teaching is summarized in 1:3–11, which

is in form a miniature homily, following a pattern used in farewell speeches. It plays a key role in the book, as a definitive summary of Peter's ethical and religious instruction. Then there are also two passages of prophecy (2:1-3a; 3:1-4) in which Peter foresees that, after his death, his message will be challenged by false teachers.

The rest of 2 Peter is structured around these four passages belonging to the testament genre. It includes three apologetic sections which aim to answer the objections the false teachers raise against Peter's teaching. There are four such objections, but only the last of them is explicitly stated as such (3:4). In the other three cases, the objection is implicit in the author's denial of it (1:16a, 20; 2:3b). These apologetic sections give the work its polemical character, as not simply a testamentary *statement* of Peter's message but also a *defense* of it against objections. They make it important to take account of the polemical aim of the letter when we try to appreciate its teaching. Finally, there are two passages (E^1, E^2) which contrast the libertine behavior of the false teachers (denounced in 2:10b-22) with the holy living expected of the readers if they are faithful to Peter's teaching (3:11-16).

Authorship and date

The problem of the authorship of 2 Peter is best considered in connection with the form and structure of the letter. In the Jewish literature of the time, testaments were *pseudepigraphal*. They were attributed to Old Testament figures long dead and were probably understood to be exercises in historical imagination, putting into the mouth of these figures the kind of thing they might have been expected to say. This establishes an initial presumption that 2 Peter is likewise a work written in Peter's name by someone else after his death.

It remains possible that the testament genre could have been used by Peter to write his own, real testament. But it should also be noticed how the predictive character of the testament genre is used in 2 Peter. Instead of reflecting the situation in which Peter is said to be writing, the whole work is addressed to a situation after Peter's death. His two predictions of false teachers function as pegs on which is hung the apologetic debate with these teachers about the validity of Peter's message. Moreover, whereas the testamentary passages speak of the false teachers in the future tense, predicting their rise after Peter's death (2:1-3a; 3:1-4; cf. 3:17), the apologetic sections and the denunciation of the false teachers refer to them in the present tense (2:3b-22; 3:5-10,16b).

It is difficult to read 2 Peter without supposing the false teachers to be contemporaries of the author, with whom he is already in actual debate. The alternation of predictive and present-tense references to them is therefore best understood as a deliberate stylistic device by which the author conveys the message: These apostolic prophecies are now being fulfilled. In other words, Petrine authorship is a fiction, but it is one which the author does not feel obliged to maintain throughout his work. In that case, it must be a deliberately *transparent* fiction, a literary convention which the author expected his readers to recognize as such, just as modern readers are not likely to mistake a historical novel for factual history.

For these and other reasons, most modern scholars consider 2 Peter to be pseudepigraphal, though some still defend Petrine authorship. The most cogent additional reasons for denying Peter's authorship are the Hellenistic religious language and ideas and the evidence for dating the work after Peter's death in the mid-sixties. Scholars differ widely on the date of 2 Peter, which many consider to be the latest New Testament writing. But the clearest evidence for a postapostolic date is 3:4, which indicates that the first Christian generation has died. This passage may well suggest that the letter was written at the time when this had only just become true, ca. A.D. 80–90. This was the time when those who had expected the Parousia during the lifetime of the apostolic generation would face the problem of the nonfulfillment of that expectation, but there is no evidence that this continued to be felt as a problem in the second century.

If 2 Peter was written not by Peter, but after his death, why did the author present his work in the form of Peter's testament? Probably because his intention was to defend the apostolic message in the period after the death of the apostles (cf. 3:4) against teachers who held that, in important respects, the teaching of the apostles was now discredited. Whereas they were claiming to correct the apostles' teaching, the author of 2 Peter regards it as normative for the postapostolic church.

By writing in Peter's name he claims no authority of his own, except as a faithful mediator of the apostolic message, which he defends against attacks. The form of the letter as an apostolic testament is therefore closely connected with its apologetic purpose as a vindication of the normative authority of the apostolic teaching. That the author chose to write Peter's testament is probably best explained if he was a leader of the Roman church, which had counted Peter as the most prestigious of its leaders in the previous generation.

Thus, in my view, the pseudepigraphal device expresses a justified claim by the real author to be faithfully transmitting the tradition of apostolic teaching and appropriately reinterpreting it for the new circumstances of postapostolic churches. There may be some readers who are not convinced by this approach and prefer to think of 2 Peter as a letter written by the apostle himself shortly before his death in A.D. 64 or 65. They will find that while my own view of the authorship of the letter very occasionally affects the argument of the following chapters, for the most part it makes little difference.

The opponents

The opponents have usually been identified as Gnostics; but this identification, as recent scholarship recognizes, is insecure. The only features of their teaching which are clear from our author's refutation of it are eschatological skepticism and moral libertinism. The Parousia had been expected during the lifetime of the apostles, but the first generation of Christians had now passed away. In the opponents' view, this proved the primitive Christian eschatological hope to have been mistaken (3:4, 9a). There would be no eschatological judgment (2:3b), no divine intervention to eliminate evil and establish a world of righteousness. This attitude seems to have been based on a rationalistic denial of divine intervention in history (cf. 3:4b) as well as on the nonfulfillment of the Parousia prophecy. But it was also related to the ethical libertinism of the opponents. They claimed to be emancipating people from fear of divine judgment and therefore from conventional Christian morality (cf. 2:19a). Evidently, they felt free to indulge in sexual immorality and sensual excesses generally (2:2, 10a, 13-14, 18).

This teaching involved a critique of the traditional teaching inherited from the apostles. The opponents claimed that the apostles had simply invented the idea of the Parousia (1:16a) and denied the inspiration of the eschatological prophecies of the Old Testament (1:20-21a). Depending on the correct interpretation of 3:16b, they either appealed to Pauline teaching about freedom in support of their libertine views or they believed Paul's expectation of the imminent Parousia discredited his teaching.

There is no basis in 2 Peter itself for supposing that these teachings of the opponents had a Gnostic basis. They are more plausibly attributed to the influence of popular pagan attitudes. The false teachers probably aimed to disencumber Christianity of elements which seemed to them an embarrassment in their pagan cultural environment: its apocalyptic eschatology, always alien to Hellenistic thinking and especially embarrassing after the apparent failure of the Parousia hope, and its ethical rigorism, which contrasted awkwardly with the permissiveness of pagan society. From a general familiarity with Hellenistic religious debate, they were able to deploy current skeptical arguments about eschatology and divine revelation. They may have seen themselves as rather daring radicals trying to clear a lot of traditional nonsense out of the church.

In response to this challenge, the author of 2 Peter mounts a defense of the apostolic expectation of judgment and salvation at the Parousia, and of the motivation for righteous living which this provides.

His definitive summary of Peter's teaching (1:3-11) already stresses the need for moral effort if eschatological salvation is to be assured. This positive statement is then backed up by apologetic arguments in the rest of the letter. The author argues that the apostles' preaching of the Parousia was soundly based on their witnessing of the transfiguration, when God appointed Jesus to be the eschatological judge and ruler (1:16-18), and on the divinely inspired prophecies of the Old Testament (1:19-21). Old Testament examples prove that divine judgment *does* happen and prefigure the eschatological judgment (2:3b-10a). As God decreed the destruction of the ancient world in the Flood, so he has decreed the destruction of the present world in the fire of his eschatological judgment (3:5-7, 10). The problem of the delay of the Parousia is met by traditional arguments drawn from Jewish tradition. The delay is long only by human standards, not in the perspective of God's eternity.

It should be seen as God's gracious withholding of judgment so that sinners may repent (3:8-9). Such arguments enable the author, at a time when the hope of the Parousia had become problematic, not to let it fade by postponing it indefinitely, but vigorously to reassert the traditional Christian hope and its relevance. Throughout his work, he is concerned that the hope for the vindication and establishment of God's righteousness in the future (cf. 2:9; 3:7, 13) necessarily motivates the attempt to realize that same righteousness in Christian lives (3:11, 14).

Theological character

The peculiar theological character of 2 Peter lies in its remarkable combination of Hellenistic religious language and Jewish apocalyptic ideas and imagery. On the one hand, for example, the author summarizes Peter's teaching in a passage which, in its ethical and religious terminology, is perhaps the most Hellenistic in the New Testament (1:3–11), though the Hellenistic language is carefully controlled by the Christian content. On the other hand, he accurately and effectively reproduces Jewish apocalyptic ideas, especially in 3:3–13.

This combination of theological styles is explained by the author's intention of *interpreting* and *defending* the apostolic message in a postapostolic and Hellenistic cultural situation. When he states the Christian message positively (1:3–11) he does so in terms which make contact with the ideals and aspirations of contemporary pagan culture. He is here engaged in the task of *translating* the gospel into terms intelligible in a new cultural environment. But this is a delicate task which requires care lest the real Christian content of the gospel be lost.

In the author's view, that was happening in his opponents' version of Christianity. In their attempt to adapt Christianity to Hellenistic culture, they were compromising essential features of the apostolic message, advocating mere pagan skepticism about eschatology and mere acquiescence in moral permissiveness. In order to *defend* the gospel against this excessive Hellenization, therefore, the author resorts to sources and ideas close to the apocalyptic outlook of the primitive church, including the letter of Jude, which is one of his sources. He sees that if Hellenized Christianity is not to become a merely paganized Christianity, apocalyptic eschatology has to be reasserted, along with the ethical motivation it provides. Second Peter thus keeps a careful balance. It offers a degree of Hellenization of the gospel message; but it protests, in the name of apocalyptic eschatology, against extreme Hellenization. The latter would dissolve the real Christian substance of the message.

Second Peter is a valuable witness to the church's difficult transition from a Jewish to a Hellenistic environment, and it provides an instructive example of the way in which the message of the gospel must be preserved through the necessary process of cultural translation.

Relationship to Jude

There are such close resemblances between certain passages of Jude and 2 Peter that some kind of literary relationship between the two works seems certain. Almost all modern scholars consider that 2 Peter has used Jude as a source. But the material common to the two letters has frequently misled scholars, as well as ordinary readers, into supposing that they must be aimed against the same opponents and reflect the same situation in the life of the early church.

In fact, careful study of 2 Peter's use of Jude shows that the author has adapted the material he derives from Jude for his own, rather different, purpose. He found Jude's letter useful because Jude was writing against opponents who promoted libertinism and because of Jude's stress on the coming judgment of such people. But the opponents the author of 2 Peter faced also had characteristics quite distinct from those of Jude: their explicit, argued skepticism about eschatology and their critique of apostolic teaching. These required a different, fuller apologetic response. Whereas Jude faced a problem that arose and could be met within the religious culture of Palestinian Judaism, 2 Peter belongs to a later church situation, where the pagan Hellenistic environment presented both a new challenge and a new opportunity for the gospel.

Themes

We shall divide the teaching of the letter into four major topics: justification and righteousness, the meaning of freedom, Christian hope, and the nature of Scripture. But we shall frequently notice that these topics are all interconnected in the argument of 2 Peter.

1 JUSTIFICATION AND RIGHTEOUSNESS

Posing the issue

The central theological issue in 2 Peter is the relation between ethics and eschatology. As we have seen, this was also an important concern of Jude's, but the issue is focused more strongly and dealt with in more detail in 2 Peter. This is because of the particular character of the false teaching which this letter opposes. The two main planks of the opponents' teaching were eschatological skepticism and ethical permissiveness. These two features were closely linked since the opponents' denial of future judgment implied, for them, the removal of moral sanctions and freedom from moral restraint. Freedom from fear of divine judgment was at the same time a liberation from moral constraint. As a result, 2 Peter's central concern is to insist on the necessary connection between the practice of righteousness in Christian life now and the attainment of eschatological salvation in the future. Christianity is "the way of righteousness" (2:21) which leads "into the eternal kingdom of our Lord and

Saviour Jesus Christ" (1:11). Progress in the way of right-eousness is, in some sense, a condition for entry into the eternal kingdom of Christ.

In order to focus our consideration of this issue, it may be useful to point out at once two theological dangers which arise in making future salvation conditional on the practice of righteousness. One of these we might call the problem of the Reformation, because it was the central issue in the debate over justification between Roman Catholics and Protestants in the sixteenth century. If final salvation is made dependent on the Christian's progress in ethical righteousness (in sixteenth-century terms, "inherent" as opposed to "imputed" righteousness), the danger, which Luther so clearly saw, is of a self-centered ethic and an anthropocentric eschatology. The pursuit of righteousness becomes self-interested—it is the means of achieving one's own salvation—and heaven exists purely in order to reward one's efforts to be righteous. At its worst, this approach makes ethics and eschatology into the instruments of the human pursuit of self-justification and self-deification.

The second danger we may call the problem of contemporary Christianity in its concern for social and political righteousness in the world. Here the danger is of an individualistic pursuit of one's own ethical righteousness in order to inherit salvation in the next world. Eschatology becomes the means of assuring pious Christians that they will be rewarded for their piety while their godless neighbors will get their deserved punishment in the end. Again the connection between ethics and eschatology degenerates into a self-interested distortion of both. The two dangers are not unconnected, of course, and they come together in the devastating critique of 2 Peter which was launched in a famous, influential essay by the Lutheran scholar Ernst Käsemann.[1] For Käsemann, 2 Peter succumbs to both these dangers, and he therefore sees it as a prime example of Christianity's lapse from the Pauline gospel into "early Catholicism." This criticism does not do justice to 2 Peter, but it is worth bearing in mind because it raises important questions about the theology of 2 Peter.

Ethics and eschatology in 1:3–11

This passage plays a key role in 2 Peter. As we can see from the reference to it in 1:12, 15, it is a summary of the apostolic message which Peter bequeaths to the church as his testament. As such it is the fundamental *positive* statement about the relationship of ethics and eschatology which the rest of 2 Peter then aims to defend against the opponents' objections. It is also relevant to remember that this passage is the best example of our author's translation of Christianity into Hellenistic religious language.

These verses follow a standard homiletic pattern, which consists of three sections:

(a) a historical/theological section, which recalls the acts of God in salvation history (vv 3–4);

(b) ethical exhortations, based on (a) and with (c) in view (vv 5–10);

(c) an eschatological section, in which salvation is promised and judgment threatened (v 11).

This formal structure embodies a theological structure of thought. The ethical exhortations of the central section (vv 5–10) are framed by the saving act of God in the past (vv 3–4) and the prospect of salvation or judgment in the future (v 11). The saving act of God in the past is the *basis* for the ethical behavior expected of the readers, while the eschatological prospect provides a *motive* for ethics. To move from the salvation experienced in the past to the salvation which can be finally attained in the future one must pass

Justification and Righteousness

through the central section—ethical progress in the present. In some sense, final salvation is conditional on appropriate ethical behavior—though this does not, as we shall see, mean that the latter is what actually achieves or "earns" final salvation. Thus the structure of the passage already indicates a balance between a stress on the *prevenient* saving action of God, which precedes all Christian endeavor, and, on the other hand, the need for human ethical endeavor along the way which leads to final salvation. To understand this theological structure in more detail, we need to look carefully at each of its three sections.

Prevenient grace (1:3–4)

These verses read:

His [Christ's] divine power has bestowed on us [Christians] everything necessary for a godly life, through the knowledge of him [Christ] who called us by his own glory and might, by means of which he has bestowed on us the very great and precious promises, so that through them you may escape the corruption that is in the world because of sinful desire and become sharers of the divine nature.

This sentence, which is typical of 2 Peter's rhetorical style, takes some unraveling. Christ's "divine power" and "his own glory and might" are synonymous phrases which describe the event of Jesus Christ—his incarnation, ministry, death, and resurrection—conceived in Hellenistic religious terms as a manifestation of divine power. By means of this divine saving act, Christians are said to have received four things:

First, *knowledge* of Christ ("knowledge of him who called us"). The author of 2 Peter uses two words for "knowledge" (*epignōsis*, used here and in 1:2, 8; 2:20, and *gnōsis*, used in 1:5,

6; 3:18) in different senses. *Epignōsis* is the fundamental knowledge of God in Christ which is gained in conversion and makes a person a Christian; *gnōsis* is the knowledge which can be acquired and developed in the course of Christian life. In 1:3 the reference is to the knowledge gained in conversion.

Secondly, through this knowledge Christ "has bestowed on us everything necessary for a godly life." The word translated "bestow" (*dōreisthai*), found here and in verse 4, was used especially of royal and divine bounty. It stresses the favor and generosity of God in granting us grace. So the emphasis is on salvation as gift. Though the special concern of 2 Peter is the living of a godfearing life, the author here roots the Christian's ability to live such a life in the generous, freely given grace of God in Christ. He has given us "*everything necessary for a godly life.*" We do not have to add to God's grace from our own human resources. What we have to do is to live a godly life out of the resources of divine grace which have been given us.

Thirdly, there is Christ's *calling* of Christians. Though only mentioned in verse 3, the mention is important because it is taken up in verse 10 ("confirm your call and election"). Christians have been called by Christ to be his people, but this calling has still to reach its goal in his heavenly kingdom. So between the call and its goal lies Christian discipleship in response to the call and on the way to the goal.

Finally, Christ has bestowed on us his *promises*. These are promises which Christ gave but have yet to be fulfilled. Their content, still to be attained by Christians in the future, is that believers should "escape the corruption that is in the world . . . and become sharers of divine nature." We postpone a consideration of the meaning of this description of the eschatological hope until the next chapter, but we should note here that once again what Christ has already given us (promises) points forward to a goal yet to be attained. The author now goes on to describe the way from one to the other as the ascent of a ladder of virtues.

The ladder of virtues (1:5-7)

If we compare this list with other New Testament lists of virtues, it appears distinctive in two ways: in terminology and in form. As far as terminology is concerned, although some distinctively Christian terms are included in this list ("brotherly affection," "love"), in general its ethical terms correspond much more closely to the terminology of Hellenistic moral philosophy than do other New Testament lists (with the exception of Philippians 4:8, which is also notably Hellenistic). Three terms in 2 Peter's list are markedly Hellenistic in flavor and occur only once each in other New Testament lists: virtue (*aretē*), godliness (*eusebeia*), and self-control (*enkrateia*). "Virtue" especially encapsulates the Hellenistic ethical ideal of virtue as the achievement of human excellence. Plainly, the author, in accordance with his general concern to translate the gospel into terms which make contact with its Hellenistic environment, has sought to bring the Christian ideal of the virtuous life as close as possible to the moral ideals familiar to his pagan contemporaries. But we cannot properly assess this procedure until we have considered the second difference between this and other New Testament lists of virtues: its form.

Second Peter 1:5-7 uses the literary device known as *sorites*, or chain argument. This is the structure: A . . . B, B . . . C, C . . . D (and so on), a favorite Hellenistic rhetorical device which occurs quite often in Jewish and early Christian literature. A particular type of sorites was the ethical sorites, the chain or ladder of virtues used by Stoics and other writers on ethics as a memorable summary of their view of the good life. A rabbinic example (*Mishnah*, tractate *Soṭa* 9:5) will illustrate the form:

Zeal leads to cleanliness,
and cleanliness leads to purity,
and purity leads to self-restraint,
and self-restraint leads to sanctity,
and sanctity leads to humility,
and humility leads to the fear of sin,
and the fear of sin leads to piety,
and piety leads to the Holy Spirit,
and the Holy Spirit leads to the resurrection of
    the dead.

In this example, as in some others, the chain of virtues leads to an eschatological climax (resurrection). Second Peter does not have an eschatological climax within the sorites, but the eschatological goal of the sorites follows in verse 11.

The peculiarly Christian character of 2 Peter's sorites results from the combination of two distinctive features: (a) the list begins with faith and ends with love, and (b) each virtue *derives from* the preceding one. This second feature is frequently obscured in translation.

The Greek (literally: "by means of your faith supply virtue" and so on) implies that each virtue in the list is the means of producing the next. But the difficulty of putting this nuance into an English translation which preserves the form of the sorites no doubt accounts for the inaccurate English rendering: "add to your faith virtue" (KJV), "supplement your faith with virtue" (RSV), "add to your faith goodness" (NIV). These translations are very unfortunate in relation to the issue of justification, since by introducing the idea of *adding*, which is not in the Greek, they suggest that faith needs supplementing by moral effort. They imply salvation by faith *and* works. What the sorites actually suggests, however, is that faith is the root out of which all virtues grow. It is not supplemented with virtue, but develops into virtue. The sixteenth-century mediating formula, "faith working through love" (from Gal 5:6), might be an appropriate description of the concept.

It would be a mistake to attach any significance to the order of items in the list, with the exception of the first and last (faith and love). In an ethical sorites of this sort, it is not possible to give some kind of psychological explanation of how each virtue develops out of another. The idea is simply that the virtues are interconnected, but the precise order in which they are listed is random. However, what is certainly deliberate and significant is that faith is placed first, as the root of all the virtues, and love is placed last, as their culmination.

The last virtue in a list of this kind is not simply the final or even the most important, but the virtue which *encompasses* all the others. Thus the Hellenistic elements in the list are given a decisively Christian interpretation by their place in a list of virtues rooted in Christian faith and culminating in Christian love. They witness to the fact that Christian ethics cannot be totally discontinuous with the moral ideals of non-Christian society. But the new context in which they are set ensures that they are subordinated to and are to be interpreted by reference to the comprehensive Christian ethical principle of love. Thus "self-control," for example, is not for Christians a virtue simply in itself or for the reasons it was valued in Stoicism, but because self-discipline is a necessary element in the practice of Christian love. Thus 2 Peter remains faithful, in a new context, to the central insight of Jesus' moral teaching: that love is the all-inclusive ethical principle, the requirement which sums up the whole of the Law and the prophets (Matt 22:40).

The salvific necessity of good works

The following verses (8–10) insist that the ladder of virtues must be climbed if final salvation is to be attained. The knowledge of Christ and the forgiveness of sins received in conversion and baptism lose their value unless moral progress follows. The exhortation to "make all the more effort to confirm your call and election" (v 10) does not mean, as seventeenth-century Calvinists thought, that Christians' moral progress provides them with a *subjective* assurance of their election. It means that the ethical fruits of faith are *objectively* necessary for the attainment of final salvation. The divine initiative in our calling to be Christians will not reach its goal—our entry into Christ's kingdom—unless it is ratified by our response in moral effort.

Finally, the way the eschatological goal is attained, according to verse 11, is highly significant: "in this way entry into the eternal kingdom of our Lord and Saviour will be richly provided for you." The phrase, "will be richly provided," indicates the lavish provision made by the divine generosity. Thus, while the whole passage emphatically regards the ethical fruits of faith as *necessary* to the attainment of final salvation, this phrase rules out the notion that the latter is, in any strict sense, a *reward* deserved in justice for the Christian's good works. Final salvation is the gift of God's generosity which far exceeds any human merit. In spite of the passage's stress on human participation in the attainment of salvation, it ends as it began (v 3) with an attribution of salvation to God's grace.

In summary, this passage (1:3-11) plainly presents both the priority of God's grace to all human participation and the excess of God's grace beyond all human achievement. It also makes clear that the Christians' response to God's grace in *faith* is the root from which the whole of their ethical obedience to God must grow. Within this context, however, it lays great stress on the necessity for faith to bear fruit in ethical behavior, because without it final salvation cannot be attained.

Because of this stress, the teaching of the passage is, in sixteenth-century terms, more "Tridentine" than "Lutheran." The Council of Trent's decree on justification is closer to the teaching of this passage than are the Lutheran formularies. But the reason for this correspondence must be appreciated. It lies in the *polemical* context in each case. The Council of Trent perceived in Lutheran teaching (largely mistakenly) an antinomian threat similar to that posed by the opponents in 2 Peter. In both cases, this perceived threat of antinomianism leads to a stress on the importance of good works for the attainment of salvation in the future. *As a polemical correction* this emphasis is quite justified. Second Peter, it must be admitted, lacks any stress on the scandal of the gospel as the message of God's love for sinners which accepts and welcomes the most wicked. But it emphasizes another side of the matter which must not be forgotten: the fact that God's love in the gospel does not *succeed* until it makes sinners into saints.

However, this passage (1:3-11) does not stand alone in 2 Peter. As we have noticed in the introduction to 2 Peter, it is important to recognize the balance our author achieves between Hellenistic and apocalyptic material. In this case, we must put 1:3-11, with its strongly Hellenistic flavor, alongside the little apocalypse of chapter 3. If some readers feel that the specter of a self-interested ethic and an anthropocentric eschatology still seems to linger around the former passage, it will be thoroughly dispelled by the latter.

Eschatological righteousness

Second Peter 3:11-14 again makes the link, so characteristic of 2 Peter, between ethics and eschatology, between the Christian practice of righteousness now and the hope of the new world which is coming at the Parousia. The key to this link really comes in verse 13: "we are waiting for new heavens and a new earth, in which righteousness is at home." It is very notable that the *only* feature of the new world which the author considers worthy of comment is that it will be a world in which God's will will be done. Of all the points he could have made, drawing on the prophetic promises of the eschato-logical kingdom of God, only this he considers really essential: that in the new heaven and the new earth God's righteousness will reside. Here he stands within the mainstream of Jewish and Christian eschatology, at the heart of which is the theocentric hope for the eventual triumph of God's will over all evil, the vindication and establishment of God's righteousness in his world. The same theocentric hope characterized the teaching of Jesus and is enshrined in the opening petitions of the Lord's Prayer: "Your kingdom come, your will be done on earth as in heaven."

In the apocalyptic situation—typical of the Jewish and Christian literature in which this hope comes to most powerful expression—where those who love righteousness are few and oppressed, and evil seems to be taking over God's world, the hope for the time when God's righteousness is going to triumph universally is a necessary presupposition for morality. It sustains the practice of righteousness by giving the assurance that righteousness is worth maintaining, that it is the final reality of things that must prevail, however much the present situation might otherwise suggest the opposite. Hence the false teachers' denial of this future triumph of divine righteousness really was, as the author of 2 Peter perceived, a serious undermining of Christian ethical motivation.

The theocentricity of verse 13 becomes more apparent when we notice the personification of Righteousness and the background to this in Jewish apocalyptic. There is probably an echo of Isaiah 32:16, which portrays the coming age of salvation, beyond judgment, as one in which justice will prevail: "Justice will dwell in the wilderness, and righteousness will abide in the fruitful field." From this, 2 Peter borrows not only the words, but also the thought that Righteousness, represented as a person, will no longer be a temporary and occasional visitor, but will take up permanent residence.

In view of the close association in Jewish thought between righteousness and wisdom, the apocalyptic version of the Jewish myth of personified divine Wisdom is also very illuminating for our passage. First Enoch 42 tells how Wisdom, who is at home in heaven, came down to dwell with people on earth, but could find no home on earth and so returned to heaven to make her permanent home there among the angels. Wickedness, on the other hand, found a ready welcome among human beings and dwelt with them.

The contrast here between personified Wisdom and personified Wickedness makes it clear enough that the former could equally well be called Righteousness. The story portrays the present age as an evil one in which Righteousness is unwelcome on earth. It thus sets the scene for many passages in the Parables of Enoch which portray the new age, to be inaugurated by the Son of Man, as a transformed heaven and a transformed earth in which righteousness or wisdom (the terms are used virtually interchangeably) *will* find a home on earth (e.g., 45:4-5; 46:3; 48:1; 49:1-3).

Second Peter 3:13 belongs in this tradition. Righteousness, like Wisdom, is a personified *divine* quality. In this world—the pagan environment of 2 Peter's readers—God's righteousness is not welcome and cannot be at home. But after the judgment, when evil will have been purged from the world, God's righteousness will at last find a home on earth as well as in heaven. Because the inhabitants of that world will welcome her, she will settle permanently among them.

Thus the inhabitants of that world must be people who love God's righteousness, who therefore love righteousness now, who practice righteousness now and are *impatient* for the day when injustice will end and God's righteousness prevail on earth (v 12: "waiting for and hastening the coming of the Day of God"). This is the real point of 2 Peter 3:11-14. Only someone who now wants Righteousness to dwell in the world will be able to live with Righteousness in the new world.

The link between ethics and eschatology in these verses does not produce a carrot-and-stick morality of self-interest. The only reward offered to righteousness is more righteousness: a world characterized by God's righteousness. Those who live by the hope for the universal establishment of God's righteousness in the world must be people who love righteousness *for its own sake*. Living in eager expectation of the time when God's righteousness will prevail entirely and forever, they cannot but make every effort to reflect and promote righteousness in their lives now (3:11, 14).

Thus the corollary of hoping for a world in which righteousness will dwell must be active righteousness now. Ethics and eschatology belong together because Christian living is living toward the coming of God's kingdom of righteousness; it is a practice of righteousness sustained by the hope of the universal triumph of God's righteousness; it is a promoting of righteousness which is constantly straining toward that time when God's will prevails entirely and forever.

Thus the apocalyptic perspective of hope for the coming of God's righteousness in the whole creation should dispel not only the specter of a self-interested ethic, but also that of an individualistic pietism. Those who embrace this hope should be concerned with more than their own righteousness. But to see how 2 Peter has its relevance not only to the Reformation issue of justification, but also to the contemporary Christian concern for righteousness in the world, we need to turn back to chapter 2.

Noah and Lot

The way in which the eschatological hope sustains the righteous person's practice of righteousness in an unrighteous world is given concrete illustration in 2 Peter by means of two Old Testament models of the righteous person: Noah and Lot. For these we turn to the passage 2:4–10, in which the reality of divine judgment is demonstrated by reference to three classic Old Testament examples of judgment: the judgment of the fallen angels, the Flood, and the destruction of Sodom and Gomorrah. As in Jude 5–7, on which 2 Peter is here partly dependent, these examples are not just illustrations of the principle of divine judgment; they also function as *types* of the coming judgment at the Parousia. But the author has developed an element in this typology which he did not find in Jude. The Flood and the destruction of Sodom and Gomorrah were classic examples of God's *discriminatory* judgment, in which not only the wicked are condemned, but also the righteous, however few, are spared. Hence Noah and Lot become in 2 Peter types of faithful Christians who hope for deliverance at the Parousia, but meantime must live righteously in the midst of an evil society doomed to judgment.

It is significant that in his accounts of Noah and Lot the author does not focus on aspects of their deliverance (such as the ark), but on aspects of their previous life among their evil contemporaries. He must have meant these accounts to have existential relevance to his readers, living amid the pressures of a predominantly pagan society. As models for his readers, the author seems to have deliberately chosen righteous men in worst-case situations, living almost alone in flagrantly unjust societies, standing for righteousness in situations where wickedness seemed wholly triumphant. His readers must have felt themselves a beleaguered minority in the great pagan cities. The appeal of the false teachers was, no doubt, that they offered a way of relaxing the tension by giving up the concern for righteousness. In Noah and Lot the author offers his readers people who stood faithfully for righteousness in far more extreme situations than those his readers faced. But what is even more striking about the way he portrays these models is that they not only resisted the temptation to conform to their environment, they also resisted the other temptation of righteous people in such situations: the pietistic temptation to leave the world to the devil and to cultivate their own holiness. Both men were concerned with more than their own righteousness.

In this respect, as models of righteous people in an unrighteous world, the pictures of Noah (v 5) and Lot (vv 7-8) are complementary. Noah is presented as a man who proclaimed righteousness, Lot as a man who suffered for righteousness. In the case of Noah, the author draws on Jewish traditions which represented Noah as a preacher of repentance.[2] Not content with the assurance of his own salvation in the coming judgment, Noah sought to avert the judgment from his contemporaries by turning them to righteousness. Noah was a "herald of righteousness" who made sure that the claims of righteousness did not go unheard even in a world intent on silencing them.

In the case of Lot, the extended picture of his distress (vv 7b-8) may again be based on Jewish tradition which has not otherwise survived, or it may be original to the author. In any case, the stress on this point is very significant. Lot suffers in an evil society, but not because he is a *victim* of the wicked who has personally suffered at their hands. His torment is the inner distress of a conscientious person surrounded by blatant evil and helpless to prevent it. Lot is presented as the genuinely righteous person, who loves righteousness, longs to see righteousness done in the world, and is afflicted by its absence from the world around him. He is the kind of person whose practice of righteousness, in a world where evil seems triumphant, is sustained by the hope of the triumph of God's righteousness in the future.

If 1:3-11 stood alone, it might promote a somewhat pietistic concern with one's own virtue. It is balanced, however,

Justification and Righteousness

by the apocalyptic emphasis of the rest of the letter on a theocentric concern to see God's righteousness done in God's world. Of course, the apocalyptic perspective speaks to the extreme situation, in which the righteous are powerless to prevent the evil of an overwhelmingly oppressive society. It therefore tends to set all its hopes on an imminent divine intervention to establish universal righteousness finally and forever.

The extremity of the situation and the imminent expectation naturally belong together. The more extreme the contemporary Christian's experience of injustice permeating society, the more he or she will understand this apocalyptic perspective. But not even Noah is represented as giving up on his contemporaries. People who love righteousness for God's sake will promote righteousness in society through whatever opportunity is afforded them. Their impatience for the world in which righteousness will be at home will not allow them simply to wait passively for it. But the greater the injustice they confront, the more their love of righteousness will need to be sustained by the hope that, in the end, God's righteousness will unequivocally prevail.

2 FREEDOM—TRUE AND FALSE

In the great pagan cities of Asia Minor, Christian morality, with its rigorous standards inherited from Judaism, clashed with the generally low moral standards of pagan society. The insidious attraction of the teaching of the false teachers whom the author of 2 Peter opposes was that it removed this difficulty. And it did so in the name of freedom, that immensely potent but deeply ambiguous word. "They promise them freedom" (2:19). The gospel, claimed the false teachers, has set us free from moral rules. Admittedly, the apostles who founded our churches taught us Jewish morality, but they were Jews, still under the influence of their Jewish background. They failed to see that Christ has set us free from all that. So the opponents probably argued. They could represent their message as an updating of Christianity which dispensed with old-fashioned morality and brought Christianity into line with the moral standards of their society. Their watchword "freedom" also implied freedom from the fear of judgment, and so brought their eschatological skepticism into play in the interests of moral permissiveness. Eschatological sanctions for morality—the threat of divine judgment—they dismissed as an incredible myth, invented as an instrument of social control. Christians whom Christ has set free ought no longer to be burdened with moral obligations enforced by the threat of judgment.

Animal behavior

What this vaunted freedom of the false teachers really amounts to the author of 2 Peter exposes in his long passage of denunciation (2:10b-22). A curious feature of this passage is the recurrence of references to animals, with whom the false teachers are repeatedly compared or contrasted. The theme begins in verse 12, where the author has borrowed it from Jude 10. The false teachers are like animals who live not by reason but by mere instinct. The basic thought is similar to Jude's, but the context is slightly different (vv 10b-13a)[1] and the analogy has been expanded beyond Jude's use of it. The animal stupidity of the false teachers is revealed in their attitude toward the powers of evil. In their brazenly immoral behavior they take no notice of the danger they run of falling into the grip of demonic forces and sharing their fate. In their boasted freedom they scoff at the powers of evil, confident of their immunity from judgment. But like animals, unaware that they are likely to be hunted and slaughtered, the false teachers, lacking all knowledge of the realities of good and evil, fail to see the danger they are in if they continue in immorality. They are in fact throwing in their lot with the forces of evil they scoff at, are falling into their power, and so will perish with them on the day when all evil will be eliminated from God's creation. Thus the false teachers, who think themselves so superior to more conventional believers, in fact lack all real understanding of their own situation. Their thinking is on the level of the unreasoning animals

This being so, their behavior sinks to the level of mere animal instinct. As so often happens with people who think themselves superior to moral rules, their freedom means, in practice, a life devoted to sensual self-indulgence. The picture which the author goes on to paint of the life of these people who think themselves so enlightened and so liberated is dominated by physical excess of every kind: gluttony, drunkenness, sexual immorality, and greed. Their greed (v 14) is a key point, which is developed in the comparison with Balaam (vv 15–16). These people are in the business of religious teaching in order to make a good living for themselves out of it. They expect to be supported by their followers in some style. And this is one of the roots of their distortion of the gospel, for the motive distorts the message.

Religious teachers motivated by greed will preach what people want to hear. The corruption of themselves and their message (and consequently of their disciples) may have happened only gradually as they failed to resist the temptation that comes to everyone who depends on religious teaching for his or her living. They found that an effective way to win disciples and support was to relax the rigor of the Gospel. The more they slipped into self-indulgence themselves, the more their teaching pandered to the natural tendency to self-indulgence in their hearers. Their own pleasure-seeking lifestyle became dependent on their sanctioning a similar lifestyle among their disciples. They, and their followers, became trapped in a vicious circle of mutually dependent self-interest. So much for their supposed freedom!

In their greed they invite comparison with Balaam (vv 15–16), the prophet who tried to sell his services for money (Num 22). When the king of Moab wanted to hire Balaam to curse the people of Israel, Balaam at first refused because he knew this would not be God's message. But he was swayed by his greed and became willing to deliver a false prophecy. His motive distorted his message. Balaam's judgment was so affected by his greed that he actually thought he could succeed in his plan of opposing God's will. This was "madness" (v 16), comparable with the false teachers' belief that they can sin with impunity. But in Balaam's case even his donkey knew better than that! It was the donkey who told Balaam what an ass he was being. The savage humor continues to expose the level to which the false teachers have sunk by comparing them with animals. The comparison is now in the animal's favor.

The animal theme recurs at the end of the chapter (v 22), where two proverbs are quoted, one about a dog (from Prov 26:11), the other about a pig. Since the reference to a dog would not suggest pet dogs, but the packs of pariah dogs that roamed the streets scavenging, both proverbs refer to animals regarded as dirty and disgusting. The point of both is that the animal, having got rid of its filth, returns to it, apparently drawn by an irresistible attraction to dirt. Dogs have a nasty habit of vomiting and then, unable to leave things alone, returning to sniff round their vomit. The story of the sow, well-known in the ancient world,[2] was that the sow wandered into the public baths and, because pigs enjoy splashing around in water, had a good bath and left the bathhouse in a state of unaccustomed cleanliness. But as soon as she came upon an inviting patch of mud she could not resist the urge to wallow in it.

The picture illustrates the false teachers' apostasy. When they became Christians, in conversion and baptism, they washed away all the filth of their pagan past, but they are now reverting to it. They are once again wallowing in the immorality of the world as though nothing had happened to them at all. But in fact they are now in a worse state than before their conversion. In verse 20 the author alludes to the man in Jesus' story (Matt 12:43-45; Luke 11:24-26) to whom the dispossessed demon returned with seven companions more evil than itself.

Similarly, apostates like the false teachers do not simply return to their pre-Christian past, because in the meantime they "have come to know the way of righteousness." Their apostasy involves sinning with full knowledge against God's moral demands and spurning the grace which is available through Christ for holy living. The culpability is greater than that of sins committed in ignorance during their pre-Christian life. Their ignorance now—their stupid, animal-like disregard for moral categories—is no excuse because it is an ignorance they have willingly embraced in their deliberate rejection of the light they once enjoyed. The verdict is harsh, but realistic, and the only hope of their reclamation lies in such a harshly realistic exposure of their dangerous condition.

Freedom and slavery

It has become apparent that the much-vaunted freedom of the false teachers is quite illusory. They have fallen into a common trap of misunderstanding freedom as absolute autonomy. They wished to be free of any obligation to anyone or anything, free to please only themselves. But human beings are not made to be autonomous. Those who try to be end up subject to all manner of things which dominate and degrade their lives, including their own excessive physical drives and their own insatiable appetite for self-gratification. The most dedicated pursuers of selfish pleasure remain addicted to their pleasures long after they have ceased to enjoy them. The author's most significant comment on the false teachers' way of life is 2:19: "They promise them freedom, but they themselves are slaves of corruption; for 'people become slaves of whoever overpowers them.'" They promise freedom—this is the potent appeal of their teaching—but they cannot give what they promise because they themselves are slaves. In their illusory pursuit of autonomy, they have yielded themselves to sin and so become subject to Corruption (here personified as a slavemaster). The author clinches the point by quoting a common proverb: "People become slaves of whoever [or whatever] overpowers them."

"Corruption" (phthora) in verse 19 should not be understood as moral corruption, but (as in 1:4, to which we shall turn shortly) as the physical result of moral corruption: mortality. The idea of enslavement to corruption is also found in Romans 8:21, which similarly personifies phthora: "the creation itself will be set free from its bondage to decay (phthora) and obtain the glorious freedom of the sons of God." The whole of the physical world seems, in its present condition, inescapably subject to eventual physical dissolution. Sin is the self-destructive urge to consent to and to become involved in this process of destruction which is also God's judgment insofar as he allows sin to take its self-destructive course.

To this bondage to sin and death there is an alternative. Once the desire for absolute autonomy is recognized as illusory and unobtainable, we can see that the real choice is between these: alienating subjection to forces destructive of human reality and liberating obedience to the truth of human existence. The former is slavery to sin, the latter is obedience to righteousness. Each has its eschatological consequence: slavery to sin leads to destruction, obedience to righteousness leads to eternal life (see Rom 6:16-23). The latter form of obedience is not experienced as slavery, because it is in accordance with human nature and leads to the true fulfillment of human nature. It is experienced as liberation from sin and the hope of liberation from mortality. It is true human freedom, freedom not to do whatever one chooses, but the freedom freely to be what one was created to be, to fulfill oneself in right relation to God and to others (righteousness).

Although the author of 2 Peter does not describe in chapter 2 the Christian alternative to the false teachers' way of living, he suggests its character by the "way" terminology, which refers to Christianity as an ethical way of life. It is "the way of truth" or "the true way" (2:2), "the straight way" from which the false teachers have strayed (2:15), and "the way of righteousness" (v 21). Christianity is not just any way of living, and true Christian freedom is not the freedom to choose just any way of living. Christianity is a definite kind of way, the right way which leads in the right direction, the way characterized by righteousness. Christian freedom is the freedom to live in this way. It is the way that 2 Peter has described more fully in the ladder of virtues (1:5–7).

To live in the way of righteousness is also to obey Christ as Lord. This is why the false teachers, who reject the way of righteousness, "deny the Master who bought them" (2:1). This means (like Jude 4, on which it depends) that they reject his moral authority. But the word *despotēs*, which Jude uses in the sense of a ruler, 2 Peter takes in its other sense of a master of slaves and so is able to extend the image with the words "who bought them." Christ is the Master of his Christian slaves because he has bought them (at the cost of his death). The image is the rather common New Testament one of redemption as the transferral of slaves by purchase from one owner to another (cf., Acts 20:28; Rom 6:17–18; 1 Cor 6:20; 7:23; 1 Pet 1:18–19; Rev 5:9; 14:3–4). Those who were once slaves of sin are now slaves of Jesus Christ. The image, however, is paradoxical, for it involves the sense of liberation from slavery to sin. To be slaves of Jesus Christ is, in another sense, to be set free from slavery. The paradox expresses the early Christian discovery that to serve Jesus Christ is to be truly free. It is to be liberated from all that oppresses and degrades human life and to find fulfillment in glad and free obedience to the only one who can rightly claim our absolute obedience. Because we were made for God, giving ourselves wholly to anything except God is enslavement; but giving ourselves wholly to God is liberation.

Liberation from mortality

The false teachers are enslaved to mortality (2:19). Their way of life leads to final destruction. By contrast, Christ has given to Christians the promise of escaping from mortality: "so that through them [his promises] you may escape the corruption that is in the world because of sinful desire and become sharers of divine nature" (1:4). However, these words require some careful discussion.

The whole of this description of Christ's promises is couched in Hellenistic religious terminology, which the author has taken over for Christian purposes but in such a way as to make contact with the religious aspirations of his contemporary society. We must, therefore, understand it initially against the background of Hellenistic views of human destiny. The two parts of the promise—escaping corruption and sharing in divine nature—belong closely together, but it will be convenient first to consider each in turn.

"The corruption [phthora] that is in the world" is not moral but physical corruption: decay, transitoriness, mortality. Throughout Hellenistic religious literature is found the contrast between the incorruptibility of divine nature and the corruptibility of everything in this material world, including the human body.

Hellenistic Jewish writers in the Diaspora had already, before Christianity, taken over this contrast and used it in expressing the Jewish hope of eternal life beyond death in terms intelligible in the cultural world of their time. The contrast was also used by Paul (cf., 1 Cor 9:25), who saw the whole of this world in bondage to corruption (Rom 8:21) and Christians as awaiting the eschatological gift of incorruptibility (1 Cor 15:42, 52-54; Gal 6:8). The Christian hope, then, as 2 Peter 1:4 puts it, is to escape mortality by the gift (whether at death or at the Parousia is not clear) of an immortal form of life.

However, we should notice very carefully the phrase "because of sinful desire," which significantly modifies the typical Hellenistic view of the matter. In Greek thought, it is simply the materiality of this world which accounts for its decay and mortality. Our plight is our entanglement in the physical world, and immortality is possible only by escape from the physical. Genuinely moral considerations are irrelevant—or at least subordinate to the fundamental problem of materiality. But 2 Peter 1:4 attributes mortality not to materiality as such, but to sin. "Sinful desire" is the root cause of evil, through which mortality has entered the world (cf. Eph 4:22).

The escape from mortality is the negative side of the coin, of which the positive is becoming "sharers in divine nature." The phrase must be understood with reference to its origin in a Hellenistic religious context. There "divine nature" does not refer to the nature of the one God but to the nature of the gods, the immaterial beings of the divine world. Hellenism divided reality into this material world, which is corruptible by nature, and the immaterial, divine world, which is incorruptible, immortal by nature. Not only the one supreme God but all the many other immortal beings participate, in this sense, in divine nature. Human nature straddled the two worlds. Its physical part, the body, belonged to the corruptible world; its spiritual part, the mind, belonged to the immortal world of the gods. The aspiration of much Hellenistic philosophy and religion was for the soul to escape its involvement in this corruptible world and recover its true, godlike nature, participating in the immortality of the gods.

Diaspora Judaism had already taken over the terminology of this way of thinking in order to express its own religious tradition in terms appropriate to its Hellenistic environment. When Jewish writers spoke of human destiny as "divinization" and "sharing in divine nature," they were using such language in a way consistent with Jewish monotheism. They did not mean that human beings become in any proper sense "gods," still less that they are absorbed into the nature of the one God. But they did hold that the human being, created in the image of God, is capable, by God's grace, of resembling God in his immortality and incorruption. To share in the divine nature is not to participate in the essence of the one God. It is to become immortal, to become one of those heavenly, immortal beings whom pagans improperly called "gods." At most, it means to be *like* God in his immortality.

Second Peter certainly uses this terminology in the way Jewish writers had already used it. To become sharers in divine nature is simply to receive from God the "godlike" characteristic of immortality (whether at death or at the Parousia is not specified). A stronger doctrine of "deification," such as has become characteristic of Eastern Orthodox theology, cannot be based on this text. (In a general way it has much more support from the Pauline doctrine of Christian participation in the Holy Spirit, which is by no means unconnected with the immortality of the resurrection life: Rom 8:11; 1 Cor 15:42-53.)

Second Peter has been much criticized for its use of Hellenistic religious language, as though the integrity of the gospel has been lost through translation into an alien cultural form. The language of 1:4, as a signal case of this, has been a particular target of attack. However, we have already noted that the Hellenistic dualism behind the language does not go uncorrected, even in this verse. Moreover, it is unfair to neglect the fact that this verse's expression of the eschatological hope in Hellenistic terms is significantly balanced by expression in terms of Jewish apocalyptic eschatology in chapter 3. The hope of immortality in this verse should not be divorced from the hope for the triumph of God's righteousness in 3:13.

More positively, however, the author of 2 Peter should be given credit for engaging in the necessary Christian missionary task of translating the gospel into terms which make contact with the ideals and aspirations of its non-Christian context. The risks involved in this task have to be taken if the gospel is to mean anything to its hearers. The Hellenistic world's aspiration to godlike immortality was by no means completely alien to the Christian gospel's promise of eternal life in Christ. It was right that it should not be denied, but rather taken up and critically fulfilled in the Christian message of the resurrection. The modern evangelist needs, in the same way, to identify contemporary non-Christian aspiration to human fulfillment and to show how the good news of Jesus Christ meets people in these aspirations. Such aspirations fundamentally arise from human nature created in the image of God though, of course, they take varying forms in different human cultures. They are all incomplete. But they provide at least an initial point of entry into the relevance of the gospel to human life as people experience it in a particular culture. They may be distorted by sin and need to be corrected by the gospel, but they are not fundamentally alien to the gospel.

Properly understood in its context, 2 Peter 1:4 makes the same point as Romans 6:16–23: enslavement to sin leads to eschatological destruction, but the way of righteousness leads to liberation from mortality through the divine gift of eternal life in Jesus Christ.

3 CHRISTIAN HOPE

Aspects of 2 Peter's eschatology have already been treated in the previous two chapters. In this chapter we shall focus on the author's refutation of the eschatological skepticism of his opponents. These false teachers rejected the future eschatological expectation of the early Christians. There would, in their view, be no divine intervention to bring the history of this world to a conclusion, to complete the divine purpose in history, and to establish God's kingdom forever. There would be no Parousia of Jesus Christ to judge the wicked and complete the salvation of the faithful. In some ways these teachers resembled some modern attempts to remove future eschatology from the Christian message. Part of their motivation, like that of such modern attempts, was the incredibility, as they saw it, of future eschatology in their cultural context.

But 2 Peter is written out of the conviction that future eschatology is not an inessential, culturally relative way of expressing Christian belief, which had to be abandoned when Christianity moved from a Palestinian-Jewish to a pagan-Hellenistic environment. Difficult though it was for the Hellenistic mind to accept, it was integral to the Christian gospel.

The author therefore engages in a serious debate with his opponents. He deals with a series of specific objections they raised to the Christian hope as it had been preached by the apostles. We should note that his defense of future eschatology is therefore oriented to the particular objections raised and felt by those influenced by the Hellenistic cultural context of the late first century. It will not necessarily answer all objections raised and felt by people today, but we may find it still relevant to some of them. We may also learn from the author's perception of the need to maintain the future hope as a nonnegotiable element of the Christian message, closely related to the integrity of Christian living. In this, the mainstream tradition of the church in his time and afterward followed him.

The evidence of the transfiguration

The false teachers did not dispute that the apostles had taught that Jesus Christ would come at the imminent end of history to judge the world and to establish his kingdom. So they had to argue that the apostles were mistaken in this. In fact, they argued that the apostles had invented the idea of the Parousia; it was not part of the Christian revelation which Jesus Christ had commissioned them to preach. Rather, it was their own human addition to that revelation. Thus the false teachers charged the apostles with teaching "cleverly concocted myths" (1:16), using the word "myth" in the derogatory sense it quite often had in ancient religious controversy: a story which purports to be true but is not.

The charge is that the eschatological teaching of the apostles was not what it claimed to be—prophecy inspired by God—but the fabrication of mere human cleverness, presumably for some unworthy motive. The Epicureans held that Greek stories of punishment in the afterlife had been invented as instruments of moral control, to keep people in fear. Since there are other indications that the false teachers were familiar with arguments deployed in Hellenistic religious debate about prophecy and revelation, they may have said something similar about the Christian expectation of judgment at the Parousia. This would reinforce the link they evidently made between their eschatological skepticism and their moral libertinism.

In 1:16–18 our author (writing in Peter's name) denies this charge and claims that the teaching of the apostles about the Parousia was not invented, but based on their eyewitness testimony to the transfiguration of Jesus. In other words, it was an integral part of the special teaching role of the apostles which was to testify to that of which they had been eyewitnesses (cf., Acts 1:21–22).

Modern readers may not immediately recognize how the event of the transfiguration of Jesus, as described in 2 Peter 1:17–18 (cf., the Gospel accounts in Matt 17:1–8; Mark 9:2–8; Luke 9:28–36), can be a basis for the expectation of his Parousia. The point is that the transfiguration is here understood as God's appointment of Jesus as his Messiah, his eschatological vicegerent. This office of Messiah involved the task of subduing the rebellious world to the divine rule, a task which Jesus had not yet fulfilled (cf., Heb 2:8). But if God had already appointed Jesus as the eschatological judge and king, the time must be coming when Jesus would be manifested to the world in triumphant glory. His manifestation in glory to the apostles on the mountain had been a foretaste of the glory in which he will appear on the last day.

This meaning of the transfiguration is conveyed through the author's allusions to the messianic Psalm 2, which is echoed in the words of the heavenly voice (cf., Ps 2:7) and suggested by the phrase "the holy mountain" (cf., Ps 2:6: "I have set my king on Zion my holy hill"). According to Psalm 2, God has enthroned his anointed king, the Son of God, on Mount Zion precisely in order to subdue the rebellious world to divine rule (Ps 2:8–9). If the transfiguration was God's installation of Jesus as the Messiah of Psalm 2, it must have had his Parousia directly in view.

The emphasis of the account is on the apostolic witness to the fact that *God himself* had chosen Jesus as his vicegerent, appointed him to the office, and invested him with glory for the task. The apostles had seen the glory given him by God and heard the voice from heaven declaring him the Messiah. Therefore, the apostles' expectation of the Parousia was soundly based on this divine action and declaration.

The evidence of Old Testament prophecy

The author has a second reply to the charge that the apostles simply invented the Christian hope: "Moreover, we [Peter and his fellow-apostles] place very firm reliance on the prophetic word, to which you would do well to attend, as you would to a lamp shining in a murky place, until the day dawns and the morning star rises in your hearts" (1:19). As well as the divine declaration at the transfiguration, the apostles had also, as a reliable basis for their expectation of the Parousia, the Old Testament prophecies inspired by God. Such prophecies, of course, are frequently interpreted in the New Testament as prophecies of the coming of Jesus as judge and king. We noticed some of these prophecies earlier (cf., chapter 3 on Jude) and the fact that a Parousia-related interpretation of them goes back to the earliest Christian teaching.

Rather than considering the transfiguration and the Old Testament prophecies two *distinct* bases for the apostolic expectation of the Parousia, it might be better to see them as *together* forming the basis for that expectation. The apostles knew that the prophecies referred to the Parousia of Jesus Christ because at the transfiguration God had identified Jesus as the one who was to establish his eschatological rule as predicted in prophecy. The prophecies predicted the final triumph of God's kingdom in history; the transfiguration identified Jesus as the messianic king who would accomplish that triumph.

This verse's comparison of Old Testament prophecy with a lamp shining in a dark place we shall leave for consideration in the next chapter, in the context of 2 Peter's view of Scripture.

The scoffers

In 1:19 the objection raised by the opponents is not explicitly stated, but is implicit in the author's denial of it. In 3:3-4 the opponents (prophesied by Peter before his death, now active after Peter's death) are explicitly quoted: "Where is the promise of his coming? For since the fathers fell asleep, everything remains just as it has been since the beginning of the world." This is the author's own formulation of their principal objection to the expectation of the Parousia, set out explicitly no doubt because of its importance as an argument which was carrying weight among his readers. He replies to it at length in 3:5-10.

The attitude of the false teachers is suggested by the word "scoffers" (3:3, borrowed from Jude 18). In the Wisdom literature of the Old Testament, the scoffer is the person who despises and ignores religion and morality (Prov 1:22; 9:7-8; 13:1, etc). Second Peter uses the term to describe his opponents as people who mock divine revelation. Their objection to the Christian hope is not raised in an open spirit of intellectual inquiry, but with an attitude of scorn. These people are out to discredit a teaching they consider absurd. Their attitude of cynical mockery is also conveyed by the way the author phrases the beginning of their objection, "Where is the promise of his coming?" In the Old Testament, this kind of rhetorical question is used to express skeptical scoffing at the convictions of believers (e.g., Ps 42:3, 10; 79:10; Jer 17:15; Mal 2:17).

The core of their objection is that the apostolic prophecy of the Parousia has been disproved by the lapse of time. They point out what has become generally known to modern scholars as "the delay of the Parousia." The Parousia had been expected during the lifetime of the first Christian generation. Indeed, the reported sayings of Jesus seemed to predict this (Mark 9:1; 13:30; John 21:22–23). But that generation ("the fathers") had now passed away, and still nothing had happened. Thus the expectation of the Parousia had not been fulfilled within the allotted time span, and so could be considered disproved. This objection probably reflects what for a period in the late first century, when people would be likely to have considered the first generation of Christian believers now passed, was an acute problem for the Christian hope until it was successfully surmounted and forgotten. The false teachers were no doubt able to exploit a genuine source of perplexity for 2 Peter's readers, as is shown by the serious attempt the author makes to meet the problem.

However, the last phrase of verse 4 reveals a further dimension to the skepticism of the false teachers. Since the death of the first generation, they maintained, everything remains unchanged—just as it has done since the beginning of the world. It seems that the failure of the Parousia hope only confirmed the opponents' assumption that divine interventions in history do not happen. The course of the history of the world has always continued, they thought, without catastrophic acts of divine judgment to disrupt its natural course. There was no reason to expect that the future would be any different. This rationalistic assumption about the uniformity of history and nature probably contributed as much to their eschatological skepticism as did the delay of the Parousia. It brings their objection close to some difficulties modern Christians may have with traditional eschatology in view of our scientific understanding of the universe.

Indeed, the whole objection, as formulated in 2 Peter 3:4, sounds remarkably similar to a famous statement of the modern theologian Rudolf Bultmann, explaining one reason why he was convinced that the message of the New Testament needed to be "demythologized" in order to be made intelligible to modern people:

> The mythical eschatology is rendered fundamentally obsolete by the simple fact that the *Parousia* of Christ did not immediately take place, as the New Testament expected, but that World-history went on, and, as every responsible person is convinced, will continue to go on.[1]

What Bultmann calls "the modern scientific world view" allows for no end to history—or at least for no theologically significant end to history.

The sovereignty of God's Word

The part of the scoffers' objection which the author tackles first is their rationalistic assumption of the necessary stable continuance of the world without divine interruption. Their confidence that the world will continue unchanged indefinitely is based on no more solid basis than the claim that it always has continued unchanged. The author shatters this facile rationalism with his belief that the world, and its continuance as a stable habitation for humanity, are radically contingent on the will of God.

His evidence is that the world was brought into existence by divine decree (3:5), and by divine decree ("the word of

God") was again destroyed in the Flood (3:6). He describes these events in terms of the ancient Jewish cosmology reflected in the Genesis accounts, according to which, at the creation, the world—sky ("heavens") and earth—emerged out of a primeval ocean (Gen 1:2, 6–7, 9). Creation was the establishment of a habitable space within the primeval chaos. The world exists because the waters of chaos—which are now above the firmament, beneath the earth, and surrounding the earth—are held back by the divine decree and can no longer engulf the world. (So the world can be said to have been "created out of water and by means of water by the word of God," v 5.)

But the potential of the waters of chaos to engulf and destroy the world is restrained, not abolished. That this is so was demonstrated in the Flood, when God decided that his creation had been so ruined by sin that he would wipe the slate clean, as it were, and make a fresh start with the one remaining righteous man and his family. According to Genesis 7:11, the waters of chaos, which had been confined at the creation above the firmament, poured through the windows of the firmament to inundate the earth. The Flood was a kind of reversion of the world to primeval chaos in order for it to be remade.

The world exists by divine decree and has already been once destroyed by divine decree. It is therefore not unreasonable to believe the word of God which has already decreed, in prophecy, that the world will be destroyed once more (v 7). In stating that this (eschatological) destruction will be by fire, the author follows a common Jewish view of his time, which held that there are two universal judgments—one in the past by water (the Flood), the other in the future by fire. This scheme of cosmic history, while not as such taught in Scripture, was deduced from the Genesis account of the Flood (along with God's promise, after the Flood, never again to destroy the world by flood) and from the prophecies of eschatological judgment by fire (e.g., Isa 34:4; 66:15–16; Zeph 1:18; Mal 4:1).

Following this scheme, our author, like many of his contemporaries, sees cosmic history divided into three great periods: the world before the Flood, the present world which will end in the eschatological conflagration, and the new world to come (3:13). There are, as it were, three events of creation: the initial creation, the unmaking and recreation of the world in the Flood, and the unmaking and recreation of the world in the fire of the final judgment. The argument is therefore that, since God created the world initially and has already destroyed and recreated it once, in the Flood, we can believe his promise that he will destroy and recreate it again in the future.

The form of this argument may initially make it seem of little value for the modern reader. The author clearly uses cosmological ideas current in his time which must now be regarded as mythological—in other words, they are evocative symbols, rather than literal descriptions of historical events.

But if we look for what was being expressed in these symbols, we shall find something still valid today. The essential point is that the continuance of the world as a habitable space for humanity cannot be taken for granted, as though nothing could conceivably interrupt it. In very early times, humanity was more at the mercy of natural catastrophes than in later historical periods, and people were probably more aware of the potential of the forces of nature to overwhelm and obliterate human history. They knew that the continuance of the world as an environment for human life ultimately depended on God's will restraining these forces.

The depiction of the Flood as an unmaking of creation, a universal reversion to chaos, is more than a picturesque way of describing whatever we may or may not find it possible to believe "actually happened" in some prehistoric natural catastrophe. It is a most powerful expression of this awareness that the catastrophically destructive potential of nature is held in check only by God's will. The stability of the world as we now experience it is no guarantee in itself that it will continue indefinitely. It is radically contingent on God's will. The idea of the two universal destructions—by water and by fire—makes a further point: that God's will for his creation is not for its indefinite continuance as it is. This is because he intends the elimination of evil from his world. So endemic is evil in the world as it is, that creation must pass through the fire of his judgment and be renewed before it is a world fit for righteousness to dwell in (3:13). The difference between water and fire perhaps suggests that future judgment will not be simply the same kind of thing as the Flood was believed to be. It will be a much more radical renewal of creation, since the Flood eliminated evil from the world only temporarily, whereas the judgment to come will remove all potential for evil from God's creation forever.

We need to try to grasp the essential point which these verses convey in a mythological way. But we cannot do so by means of the kind of "demythologization" which Bultmann applied to New Testament theology in general, i.e., by removing any reference to the world of human history and nature. These verses teach precisely the contingency of that world—not just the existential world of human inner subjectivity—on the will of God, and his intention to fulfill his purpose for that world, his creation. It is in human history precisely in its inextricable involvement with the natural world that God will act to judge and renew.

Alien as the cosmology of these verses is to us, the essential point is not alien to a modern understanding of the universe. We know very well that the continuity of an environment in which humanity can survive and flourish is not to be taken for granted, as though nothing could interrupt it. The forces of nature retain their appalling potential to interrupt and obliterate human history, while modern humanity faces the additional threat of our own newly acquired power to use the forces of nature to destroy ourselves. Although the eschatological conflagration to which verse 7 alludes must be understood as an *image*, not a literal description, of the eschatological judgment, it is an image which remains powerful today, evoking both the threat of nuclear holocaust and the eventual reabsorption of our planet into the expanding sun. These thoroughly scientific possibilities of reversion to chaos remind us of the contingency of human history in this world. They may help to refute our modern equivalents of the false teachers' facile rationalistic assumption that the world can be counted on to continue just as it always has done. But only by provoking a *religious* awareness that human history in this world is contingent *on the will of God* can they show us the credibility of the Christian hope.

Thus there is no value in a literalistic identification of the eschatological conflagration of 2 Peter with nuclear holocaust or some other destructive possibility within the horizon of our scientific view of the universe. Our author is not interested in predicting mere physical catastrophe. In his biblical perspective, human history is not at the mercy of chance or futility. The God who created the cosmos out of chaos is in sovereign control of the forces of chaos. The fire is the fire of God's moral judgment. Even that judgment is not an end in itself; it is for the sake of the new world of righteousness which he will once again create out of chaos.

The fire of judgment

Since we have just suggested that the image of fire should not be taken literally, it will be useful to look in more detail at the description of the final judgment in 3:10, 12, before turning to the second stage of the author's reply to the scoffers.

In both 3:7 and 3:10, the fire is described as affecting the physical world and as effecting judgment. In 3:7 it is "the heavens [i.e., the sky] and the earth" which are reserved for fire, but this cosmic conflagration will mark "the day of judgment and destruction of ungodly people." In 3:10, the physical destruction of the sky is clear ("the heavens will pass away with a roar, the heavenly bodies will be dissolved in the heat"), as it is also in 3:12 ("the heavens will be dissolved in flames and the heavenly bodies melt in the heat").

That this picture of the physical dissolution of the sky is also a picture of the judgment of human beings is less clear only because of the textual problem at the end of verse 10. In my commentary I have argued that we should accept the difficult but well-attested reading, *eurethēsetai*, giving the translation: "the earth and all the works in it will be found," and understand this to mean that the earth, the scene of human wickedness, and all the deeds of human wickedness committed in it will be discovered by God ("will be found" is a "divine passive" with a judicial sense). In other words, the earth and its inhabitants, with their evil deeds, will be made manifest before God and his judicial scrutiny.[2]

To this we should add the probable significance of the phrase "with a roar" (*rhoizēdon*) earlier in the verse. Though this could describe the roar of the flames which consume the sky, it is more likely a reference to the thunder of the divine voice, which is a standard element in theophany descriptions (cf., Ps 18:13–15; 77:18; 104:7; Joel 3:16; Amos 1:2). Like the "divine passive" at the end of the verse ("will be found," meaning "God will find"), it is a reverentially oblique way of indicating that the whole verse really describes the coming of the divine Judge to judgment. When the wrathful voice of God thunders out of heaven and the fire of his judgment sets the sky ablaze, the firmament and the heavenly bodies will dissolve in flames, and the earth, the scene of human wickedness, will be exposed to his wrath. Then it will be impossible for the wicked to hide from God's judicial scrutiny. They and their evil deeds will be discovered by him and condemned.

Once this meaning of the verse is seen, it becomes clear that physical destruction of the world is ancillary to the event of God's judgment of the wicked. Moreover, the nature of the physical description is determined by a prescientific picture of the world in which the sky, with the heavenly bodies in it, is the physical barrier which intervenes between God, who dwells above the sky, and the earth, which the wicked inhabit. Clearly, we cannot take the physical description literally, and we may legitimately wonder how far the author did. His concern was to evoke a picture of divine judgment rather than to predict its physical form.

This is not to say that the end of the history of this age will not involve the material world of nature. Human history, including human evil, is too inextricably involved with the natural world for that to be conceivable. It seems that the author of 2 Peter, like some other biblical writers (cf., Rom 8:21; Rev 21:1), did expect the natural world to be radically recreated. It is surely not only their righteous human inhabitants that make the new sky and the new earth (3:13) "new." But how this new creation of the world will take place we cannot imagine and the author of 2 Peter cannot tell us.

The delay of the Parousia

In 3:8–9 the author responds to the most prominent and disturbing element in the opponents' case for rejecting the traditional Christian hope: that the Parousia was expected within the lifetime of the first Christian generation, and this expectation had not been fulfilled. The author's response is not new. He takes up two arguments which had already been used by Jewish writers. Of course, these writers had not faced the specific Christian problem of the Lord's apparent failure to come within the expected period, but they had faced the recurrent problem of the delay of the Jewish eschatological expectation.

During the period in which Jews had been expecting the final intervention of God to fulfill his purposes in history, to save his people and judge the wicked, the end was always expected soon. This was entirely natural. Hope for the end always arose out of a specific situation in which people felt that the evil of the contemporary world cried out for God's intervention to end it and finally establish his righteous kingdom. Eschatological hope is naturally impatient. It was the same in early Christianity. Those who had seen God's final acts of salvation so dramatically begun in the life, death, and resurrection of Jesus, and the coming of the Spirit, naturally expected the process to reach a rapid conclusion. The arrival of God's kingdom was underway; surely its final triumph would be soon. Those who lived in the excitement of the beginnings of the Christian movement felt themselves to be living in the beginnings of the eschatological kingdom itself. Naturally, they were impatient to see it come in power and assumed they themselves would live to do so.

However, the Jewish hope had already survived a long period of disappointing delay. It had done so without any loss of the sense of imminence, but it had done so by evolving a characteristic tension between the sense of the imminence of the end and an acknowledgment and partial understanding of its delay. Two of the ways in which Jewish apocalyptic thought had already sought to understand God's delay in fulfilling his final purpose for history are taken over by the author of 2 Peter in 3:8-9.

In the first place, God, who determines the time of the Parousia, does so from a different perspective on time than that of men and women. This point is made by an allusion to Psalm 90:4, "For a thousand years in thy sight are but as yesterday when it is past." The allusion shows that, since God is not limited by a human life span but surveys the whole course of history, periods which by human standards are of great length may, from his perspective, be very short. Those who complain of the delay of the Parousia, impatient to see it in their own lifetime, are limiting the divine strategy in history to the short-term expectations of human beings. But God's purpose transcends such expectations. Thus the false teachers' accusation, that it is now too late for the Parousia to be expected, is based on their own evaluation of "lateness," not on God's.

Of course, the figure of a thousand years is not meant to give some new chronological indication of the period before the Parousia. The point is simply that a delay which seems to us very lengthy may not be so significant within the total perspective on the course of history which God commands. The author is not dispelling the imminent expectation (he continues to speak as though his readers will live to see the Parousia: 1:19; 3:14). He is not indefinitely postponing the Parousia, as though it need no longer be realistically expected. His readers are to live in continual readiness for the Parousia (3:14), which will come unexpectedly, like a thief (3:10), as Christians had always said of it. But they are not to be disturbed because it has not come within any specific period. Because God alone surveys the whole of history, he retains the date of the end in his own knowledge and power, and it cannot be anticipated by any human calculation.

However, the author does more than appeal to the wise but unknowable sovereignty of God over the times. He also offers, in verse 9, some insight into the reason why God has, from the human perspective, deferred the end—an insight which is surely not intended as a complete explanation of the matter, but as some help toward living with the delay. The delay is a respite which God has graciously granted his people before his intervention in judgment. It derives from one of the fundamental attributes of God, his forbearance, which characterizes God as "slow to anger" (Exod 34:6), mercifully deferring his judgment so that sinners may repent and escape condemnation. God delays the Parousia because he is not willing that any of his Christian people should perish. (The actual referent of "any" and "all"—in the words: "it is not his will that any should perish, but that all should come to repentance"—is the same as that of "you" earlier in the verse and, therefore, certainly limited to Christians. This is because the author wishes to turn this teaching in a practical direction: his readers should take advantage of this respite, as he urges in verses 14-15. But, of course, the *principle* enunciated here can be validly extended to God's desire that all people should come to repentance and salvation.)

Understood in this light of God's mercy, the delay of the Parousia should not be a matter of complaint. On the contrary, 2 Peter's readers, especially those whom the false teachers have enticed into sin, should take advantage of the opportunity to repent. And lest anyone should think that sinners can presume on God's forbearance, taking advantage of the delay by *not* repenting, the author immediately stresses (v 10) that God will not defer his judgment indefinitely. As Jesus' parable had made clear (Matt 24:43-44; Luke 12:39-40; cf., 1 Thess 5:2; Rev 3:3; 16:15), the day of judgment will come upon sinners with the unexpectedness of a burglar breaking in while the householder sleeps.

Second Peter's arguments must have helped the church, along with other considerations, to surmount the problem of the delay of the Parousia. They could now see that the temporal element in the first Christians' expectation of the Parousia within their own lifetime was really quite incidental to the substance of their hope. The hope itself is essential to Christian faith because it is inconceivable that the biblical God, if he is God, will not eventually achieve his purpose of overcoming all evil in his world. In the hope for the world in which righteousness will be at home (3:13) not only the truth of God's promises, but his goodness and his power, are at stake.

The problem of the delay of the Parousia is in the end a form of the problem of evil, in which also the goodness and power of God are at stake. It is: why does God continue to tolerate evil in his world and not bring about his kingdom now? Our answers to this problem of eschatological delay are necessarily as fragmentary as our answers to the problem of evil. Indeed, in neither case do we ever achieve real answers. We only find ways of living faithfully and hopefully with the problem until God himself answers it in fulfilling his promises. Meanwhile, we cannot abandon the hope for the world in which God's righteousness will be at home without abandoning faith in God's righteousness itself. To abandon that hope, as the author of 2 Peter saw very well in his conflict with the false teachers, is to undermine the struggle for righteousness in God's world now.

4   SCRIPTURE

Second Peter is unique among the New Testament documents in that it includes explicit comment on the nature of both Old and New Testament Scriptures. We shall take the three relevant passages (1:19; 1:20–21; and 3:15–16) in turn.

The value of Old Testament prophecy (1:19)

We have already seen, in the preceding chapter, how this verse fits into the author's argument against the false teachers. Against their charge that the apostles had invented their teaching about future eschatology, the author argues that the apostles ("we") based their hope for the future soundly on Old Testament prophecy: "we place very firm reliance on the prophetic word, to which you would do well to attend, as you would to a lamp shining in a murky place, until the day dawns and the morning star rises in your hearts."

In the simile of the lamp in the darkness, the author compares the world in its present condition to a place that is shrouded in darkness during the nighttime, whereas the age

97

to come (which the advent of Jesus Christ in glory will inaugurate) will be like the day which dawns after the night-time and floods the place with light. Prophecy is like a lamp that gives enough light for tasks which need to be performed during the night, but which becomes superfluous when daylight arrives. Just as the arrival of day is heralded by the appearance of the morning star, Venus, which accompanies the first glimmerings of the dawn, so the appearance of Jesus Christ himself in his messianic glory will signal the dawn of the eschatological day, the "day of eternity" (3:18) which will never end. (For Jesus as the morning star, cf., also Revelation 22:16, which, like this passage, probably alludes to the prophecy of the messianic "star" in Numbers 24:17.)

The darkness of the present world is its ignorance of God. Prophecy is a lamp in this darkness because it is a provisional, partial revelation of God. It points forward in hope to the full revelation of God which will be possible for the first time at the Parousia and will characterize the age to come. The author locates this eschatological revelation in the *hearts* of his readers ("until the day dawns and the morning star rises in your hearts"), but not because he is denying that the Parousia will be an objective, cosmic event. He is concerned here with only one aspect of the Parousia. His point is that for believers, who now live by the light of prophetic Scripture, the Parousia will mean that such light will be superseded by the full revelation of God in Christ flooding their hearts.

It is worth noting that this understanding of prophetic *Scripture* is parallel to the understanding of the transfiguration as a prophetic *event* in the preceding verses (1:16–18: see the discussion of this passage in chapter 3). The transfiguration of Jesus was a preliminary glimpse of the divine glory in which he will appear on the last day; it is therefore a *prophecy* pointing forward to that full revelation. Similarly, prophetic

Scripture gives an anticipatory glimpse of the full revelation of God and so enables us to live in hope of the latter.

When he gives this role to the "prophetic word," the author is certainly thinking primarily of actual prophecies of the Parousia and the last day, on which the apostles had based their teaching about the Christian hope. But the term "prophetic word" was used more generally for Old Testament Scripture as such. In contemporary Jewish understanding of Scripture (from which this term comes), predictive prophecy was found in many parts of Scripture besides the books known as "the prophets" (for example, in the Psalms). Moreover, the whole of Old Testament Scripture could be described as prophecy, because all its authors were spokespeople for God. Inspired by the Spirit, they conveyed God's word—just as those who were called "prophets" in the original, narrower sense did.

The Jewish understanding of Scripture as the inspired Word of God, which the church took over, had come about through applying to the whole of Scripture the analogy of prophecy. The analogy cannot be taken too strictly: the way in which other scriptural writers (such as the writers of Wisdom Literature) were inspired by the Spirit and conveyed God's Word in their writings cannot be *exactly* the same as the way the prophets were inspired and conveyed God's Word. But the extension of the category of prophecy to cover the whole of Old Testament Scripture was a way of recognizing that, in some *analogous* way, the rest of Scripture is also God's inspired Word.

Although in 1:19 the reference is primarily to prophecies which actually predict the Parousia, and so illumine our present darkness with hope, the function here ascribed to such prophecies is more broadly true of the whole of Scripture. God's revelation of himself within history, which reaches us through Scripture, is a preliminary, anticipatory revelation pointing forward to the full revelation of himself at the end of history. It is a light in the darkness; it gives real but by no means full and perfect knowledge. Our knowledge of God now is always ignorance as well as knowledge. It is enough to be going on with, like a lamp by which we can find our way in the darkness. But when we live by it, we live by faith and hope, not yet by sight (cf., 2 Cor 5:7; Heb 11:1).

This is important to remember, lest we seek in the scriptural witness to Christ a clarity and fullness of revelation which are unavailable this side of the Parousia. Unless we remember it, we shall become either disillusioned or presumptuous. Forgetting that we cannot yet live in the day of eternity, we shall either give up living toward it by the light we do have; or else we shall pretend that we do already live in it, with absurd and sometimes dangerous consequences. Thus even with regard to the Christian claim to find God's self-revelation in Scripture, an appropriate degree of Christian modesty is required.

In 1 Corinthians 13, Paul makes the same point as 2 Peter 1:19, but in different images. He contrasts the "imperfect" kind of revelation of God which is available now (in "knowledge" and "prophecy," vv 8–9) with the "perfect" revelation to come in the future (when "knowledge" and "prophecies" will therefore "pass away," vv 8–10). Then he writes: "For now we see in a mirror dimly, but then face to face. Now I know in part; then I shall understand fully, even as I have been fully understood" (v 12).

The inspiration of Old Testament prophecy (1:20–21)

The meaning of these verses is disputed. Much depends on the correct translation of verse 20, since this is a case in which translation and interpretation cannot be separated.

In my commentary I have argued in detail for the following translation of the two verses:

Above all, you must understand that no prophecy of scripture derives from the prophet's own interpretation, because prophecy never came by human impulse, but people impelled by the Holy Spirit spoke from God.

Most translations adopt a significantly different interpretation of the end of verse 20 (e.g., RSV: "no prophecy of scripture is a matter of one's own interpretation"), although the NIV is similar to my translation. The difference is fundamentally over whether verse 20 refers to the *origin* of Scripture (as in my translation and the NIV) or to the *exegesis* of scripture (as in most translations and most commentators).

In my commentary, I have argued that consideration of the context, the sequence of thought in these two verses, and the use of the same technical terminology in other Jewish and Christian writers for discussion of the inspiration of prophecy, amount to a strong cumulative argument for the translation I have given. In that case, the way that verse 20 has often been used in the past, as having something to teach us about the way we should interpret scripture, has been mistaken.

In verse 20 it is assumed that the way scriptural prophecy usually came about was that the prophet was given by God a sign (e.g., Jer 1:11, 13; Amos 7:1), a dream (e.g., Dan 7:2; Zech 1:8), or a vision (e.g., Ezek 37:1–10), which the prophet then interpreted. His prophecy, as recorded in Scripture, is therefore an interpretation of the revelation he received from God. The signs, dreams, and visions were themselves extremely obscure, and really constitute prophecy only when given an interpretation. The question then is whether this interpretation was a God-given, inspired interpretation (as the prophetic books themselves claim: e.g., Amos 7:8–9; Ezek 37:11–14) or merely the prophet's *own* interpretation, which could certainly not be relied on as correct. In the latter case, prophetic

Scripture would not be the inspired Word of God, but merely the product of the human minds of the prophets.

The false teachers were evidently claiming that this was the case. When it was said that the Christian hope for the future was soundly based on prophecies in the Old Testament, the false teachers denied that these prophecies came from God. While the prophets may indeed have received signs and dreams and visions, their prophecies were their own human interpretations of these, not God-given interpretations. They could therefore be disregarded.

In reply, the author denies this view (v 20) and goes on to explain why it is false (v 21). No prophecy in the Old Testament Scriptures, he claims, originated from human initiative or imagination ("human impulse": literally, "the will of a human being"). The Holy Spirit of God inspired not only the prophets' dreams and visions, but also their interpretations of them. When they gave these interpretations, they were "impelled" (literally, "carried along") by the Holy Spirit, so that when they spoke the prophecies recorded in Scripture they were spokespeople for God himself.

The key terms in these verses ("their own," "impelled by the Holy Spirit," "from God") had already become technical terminology in Jewish discussion of the divine origin of biblical prophecy. Our author reflects an accepted view, which was concerned to deny that the prophets of the Old Testament spoke anything that was *their own*. Rather, what they expressed was a message *from God*. They acted as God's spokespeople, it was sometimes said, just as an ambassador delivers a message which is not his own but given him by someone else. They were able to do this because they were *inspired by the Spirit*, who enabled them to discern and to convey God's message. Although this terminology represents a systematic conceptualization of the nature of biblical prophecy which was developed in the Diaspora Judaism of New Testament times, it essentially reflects the

Old Testament prophets' own understanding of the matter. In the Old Testament, false prophets are characterized as those who speak a message which is the product of *their own mind* (Jer 23:16, 26; Ezek 13:3), not received from God (Jer 23:18, 21-22). True prophets do not speak on their own initiative (cf., Jer 20:9; Amos 3:8) but, as they constantly assert, convey a message that has come to them from God.

Of course, if this understanding of prophecy is taken very strictly, it should apply only to the prophetic oracles within the Old Testament, which are explicitly spoken as "the word of the Lord." The psychological experience of the prophets, in which they were aware of receiving a message from God, would not have been the experience which lies behind the writing of most other parts of the Old Testament Scriptures. But the claim that these, too, were "inspired by God" (2 Tim 3:16) acknowledges that they also come from God and convey his message.

The Pauline letters (3:15–16)

The churches to which 2 Peter was written were located in the same area as those to which 1 Peter had been written (see 2 Pet 3:1, with 1 Pet 1:1). At least some of them must therefore have been churches founded by Paul. They would have held Paul in high esteem and regarded the letters Paul had written to them, along with any other of Paul's letters that they knew, as a theological authority. This is why our author takes the trouble to point out that his own teaching in 3:14-15a agrees with Paul's, both in the letter or letters Paul had written specifically to 2 Peter's readers and in "all his letters."

The author says that the point he has been making (that the Christian hope should be a motive for repentance and righteousness) is a point which Paul made not only in writing to 2 Peter's readers but also in all the Pauline letters he knew. It is true of most, if not all, of Paul's letters as we know them that Paul exhorts his readers to live righteously in view of the coming Parousia and judgment. So we cannot tell from this reference to its subject matter which Pauline letter (or letters) had been specifically addressed to 2 Peter's readers. But because of the location of these churches, the reference is presumably to Galatians, Colossians, Ephesians, or to more than one of these (unless we postulate Pauline letters which have not survived). What is more significant is the fact that the author knows several Pauline letters. It seems that from an early date, perhaps even before Paul's death, copies of Paul's letters circulated to churches other than their original recipients. We cannot, of course, tell how many of Paul's letters our author knew ("all his letters" means all the letters of Paul *he* knew, not all the letters of Paul *we* know!). But he must have known a collection of some letters of Paul, which presumably was used in his church.

In what the author says about Paul and his letters, we can distinguish three very significant points.

In the first place, his reference to "the other scriptures" (v 16) implies that he regards Paul's letters as Scripture and puts them in some sense in the same category as the Old Testament (since "the other scriptures" must include the Old Testament, whether or not the phrase also refers to early Christian writings other than Paul's letters). The term "scriptures" here is certainly (as always in the New Testament) used technically to refer to inspired, authoritative writings. Behind this implied use of the term for Paul's letters must lie the reading of Paul's letters in Christian worship as authoritative literature, alongside, and in the same way as, the Old Testament. As soon as Paul's letters were being treated in this way, it was natural that the same term should come to be applied to them as Christians used (following Jewish usage) for the Old Testament.

However, this certainly does not imply that there was as yet a *canon* of New Testament Scriptures, i.e., a fixed collection of authoritative apostolic writings. At this stage, in the late first century, each church would have had its own small collection of apostolic writings, which they read in worship and otherwise treated as authoritative records of the teachings of Jesus and the apostles. Such collections would have differed from church to church, and each was an open collection to which other works could be added. The process of collecting and sifting early Christian literature, which would eventually produce an agreed canon of New Testament Scriptures, was still in its early beginnings.

The second point is the author's indication of what there was about Paul's writings which enabled them to be treated as normative Christian literature, alongside the Old Testament. They too were inspired by God, as the author suggests when he says that Paul wrote "in accordance with the wisdom given to him" (v 15). "Given" is a "divine passive," meaning that God gave him wisdom, and Paul's wisdom is therefore charismatic wisdom, a gift of the Spirit. Paul's gift of wisdom (cf., 1 Cor 2:6-13) was his God-given insight into the truth and meaning of the gospel. To say that Paul's letters were written in accordance with the wisdom given him by God is really to say the same as our author had said of the Old Testament prophetic Scriptures in 1:20-21. Like the prophets, Paul did not speak out of his own wisdom, but in accordance with the wisdom given him by God. It is this that accounts for the treatment of Paul's letters as Scriptures, set alongside the Old Testament. They are authoritative writings inspired by God.

Paul himself, in 1 Corinthians 2:6-13, speaks of his teaching as embodying the wisdom given him by the Spirit. More frequently, he speaks of "the grace [*charis*] given" to him (Rom 12:3; 15:15; 1 Cor 3:10; Gal 2:9; Eph 3:2, 7; cf., Col 1:25). By this he means the gift of his apostolic commission, the divine enabling by which he receives and understands God's purpose in the gospel (Eph 3:2-10) and by which he speaks and writes with the authority of one who conveys God's message (Rom 12:3; 15:15-16). Second Peter's phrase, therefore, faithfully reflects Paul's own consciousness of his apostolic authority and charismatic inspiration.

Finally, the author condemns the false teachers' misinterpretation of Paul. In doing so, he implies something about the way to interpret Scripture correctly. No doubt the false teachers had to discuss Paul's teaching because he was a major authority in the churches where they were active. Second Peter 3:16 says that they "distort" some things in Paul's letters which are "hard to understand." This may mean that they gave Paul's teaching an unacceptable meaning and rejected it (as they did the Old Testament Scriptures), or it may mean that they misinterpreted Paul's teaching in such a way as to support their own misguided views.

In the former case, they probably interpreted Paul's statements about the imminence of the Parousia (e.g., Rom 13:11-12; 16:20; 1 Cor 7:29; Phil 4:5; 1 Thess 4:15) in such a way as to suggest that his expectations were not fulfilled and so his teaching about the Parousia had been shown to be mistaken (cf., 2 Pet 3:4). In the latter case, they may have used Paul's doctrine of justification and freedom from the law to support their antinomianism, and quoted him in support of their offer of "freedom" (2 Pet 2:19; cf., Rom 8:2; 2 Cor 3:17). There is really no way of deciding for certain whether they rejected Paul's authority or whether they claimed Paul's authority for their own views.

In either case, the author suggests that it was because they were "uninstructed and unstable" that they misinterpreted the difficult parts of Paul's letters, as well as the other Scriptures. Readers have sometimes supposed that our author himself found parts of Paul's letters hard to understand, but in fact he clearly suggests that such passages are open to misinterpretation only by "uninstructed and unstable" people. In other words, the false teachers, for all their pretensions to be teachers, had never taken the trouble to acquire a broad, sound knowledge of apostolic teaching. The passages they misinterpret in Paul are not therefore passages which are just inherently obscure and which anyone would find difficult (of course, there are such passages in Scripture), but passages which are liable to be misunderstood unless they are interpreted in the light of the rest of Paul's teaching and of the apostolic teaching generally. Without a sufficient general understanding of Christian teaching, the false teachers are not only "uninstructed" but also "unstable," i.e., likely to go astray in their interpretation of particular passages of Scripture. It follows that the way in which 2 Peter's readers will avoid being led astray and falling from their "stable position" (3:17) will be through proper and thorough instruction in the general thrust of the apostolic teaching. The most serious dangers of misinterpreting Scripture arise when we focus on individual passages without developing a broad understanding of the general teaching of Scripture.

NOTES

Jude

Introduction

1. For detailed argument to this effect, see my *Jude, 2 Peter* Word Biblical Commentary, volume 50 (Waco, Tex.: Word, 1983), and also my forthcoming book, *Jude and the Relatives of Jesus in the Early Church* (Edinburgh: T. & T. Clark).

2. For a detailed discussion, see chapter 2 of my *Jude and the Relatives of Jesus in the Early Church.*

3. For reconstruction of the story to which Jude alludes, see my *Jude, 2 Peter*, 65-76, and *Jude and the Relatives of Jesus in the Early Church*, chapter 5.

Chapter 3 Jesus the Lord

1. This chapter summarizes a full discussion of Jude's Christology in my *Jude and the Relatives of Jesus in the Early Church*, chapter 6.

2. *Jude, 2 Peter*, 43, 49, and more fully in *Jude and the Relatives of Jesus in the Early Church*, chapter 6.

3. In my commentary (*Jude, 2 Peter*, 39) I preferred the translation "Master"; but in *Jude and the Relatives of Jesus in the Early Church*, chapter 6, I have argued that "Sovereign" is more appropriate. Second Peter 2:1 ("the Master who bought them"—i.e., as slaves) takes *despotēs* in the sense of "master of household slaves."
4. Cf. Josephus, *Jewish War* 7:323, 410; *Antiquities of the Jews*, 18:23.
5. Julius Africanus, quoted in Eusebius, *Ecclesiastical History* 1.7.14.

2 Peter

Introduction
1. For the topics discussed in this Introduction, see not only my Word Biblical Commentary, but also my article, "2 Peter: An Account of Research," in *Aufstieg und Niedergang der römischen Welt*, Part II, vol. 25/5, ed. W. Haase (Berlin/New York: de Gruyter, 1988), 3713-52.

Chapter 1   Justification and Righteousness
1. E. Käsemann, "An Apologia for Primitive Christian Eschatology," *Essays on New Testament Themes*, tr., W. J. Montague, Studies in Biblical Theology 41 (London: SCM Press, 1964), 169-95.
2. Bauckham, *Jude, 2 Peter*, 250-51.

Chapter 2   Freedom, True and False
1. For the way that 2 Peter has revised Jude's reference to angels, making it into a reference to evil angels, see Bauckham, *Jude, 2 Peter*, 261-64.
2. See Bauckham, *Jude, 2 Peter*, 279-80.

Chapter 3   Christian Hope
1. Quoted in M. Werner, *The Formation of Christian Dogma*, tr. S. G. F. Brandon (London: A. & C. Black, 1957), 26.
2. Bauckham, *Jude, 2 Peter*, 316-21.

INDEX OF SCRIPTURES